Beyond Walls

Beyond Walls

*A Bicentennial History of
Bexley Hall Seabury-Western Seminary Federation*

THOMAS FERGUSON

FOREWORD BY Frank M. Yamada
AFTERWORD BY C. K. Robertson

WIPF & STOCK · Eugene, Oregon

BEYOND WALLS
A Bicentennial History of Bexley Hall Seabury-Western Seminary Federation

Copyright © 2025 Thomas Ferguson. All rights reserved. Except for brief quotations in critical publications or reviews, no part of this book may be reproduced in any manner without prior written permission from the publisher. Write: Permissions, Wipf and Stock Publishers, 199 W. 8th Ave., Suite 3, Eugene, OR 97401.

Wipf & Stock
An Imprint of Wipf and Stock Publishers
199 W. 8th Ave., Suite 3
Eugene, OR 97401

www.wipfandstock.com

PAPERBACK ISBN: 979-8-3852-4085-2
HARDCOVER ISBN: 979-8-3852-4086-9
EBOOK ISBN: 979-8-3852-4087-6

Scripture quotations are from New Revised Standard Version Bible, copyright © 1989 National Council of the Churches of Christ in the United States of America. Used by permission. All rights reserved worldwide.

Table of Contents

Foreword | vii

Introduction | xi

Chapter 1: Beginnings: Bexley Hall, 1824–1968 | 1

Chapter 2: Beginnings: Bishop Seabury Divinity School, 1858–1933; Western Theological Seminary, 1883–1933; Formation of Seabury-Western Theological Seminary, 1933 | 22

Chapter 3: Bexley Hall Seminary, 1968–2012 | 42

Chapter 4: Seabury-Western Theological Seminary, 1933–2012 | 58

Chapter 5: Bexley Seabury Seminary Federation, 2012–present | 87

Afterword | 103

Bibliography | 105

Foreword

By the Rev. Dr. Frank Yamada
Executive Director, Association of Theological Schools

SEMINARIES ARE BOTH CREATURES of context and hubs of adaptability. They are both out of necessity. They exhibit all the strains and possibilities that one would expect from institutions of higher learning that serve the changing realities of religious life in North America; and they have proven to be remarkably responsive to these shifting landscapes. Theological schools were often founded in response to the pressing realities confronting the church. As the American colonies pushed west, so too did seminaries. On other occasions, theological schools were formed because of doctrinal disagreements between different ecclesial traditions and often within a single denomination. Seminaries created distinctives—some were high church; some were low church. Some schools sought to train pastors for what was at that time the frontier. Others sought to be seminaries in the city. Today, within The Association of Theological Schools, there are schools that are residential, completely online, competency based, research focused, serving particular racial/ethnic constituencies, and seeking to serve a broad spectrum of not just Christian but also other religious affiliations, including the non-affiliated.

Because graduate theological schools are hybrid institutions, shaped by both realities within religion in North America and higher education, they are both reflections of their time and innovators. Innovation in theological schools is directly tied to how

FOREWORD

well the school is responsive to its context. Thus, seminaries both are reflective of current realities in the church and higher education and are agents of change in the broader ecology of religion in North America.

In the twenty-first century, theological schools are undergoing profound and rapid changes. They are changing in their financial and organizational model. Since 2010, there have been over fifty-five mergers and affiliations among member schools in ATS. That is a rate of a merger every three to four months. Enrollments in theological schools have been relatively flat as a collective over the past thirty years, while the number of schools has increased. Enrollments in Mainline Protestant seminaries has declined significantly. Mergers are an indicator of a large-scale consolidation. More schools with the same or decreasing number of students means that mergers will continue as we approach the end of the first quarter of the century. These shifts in the financial models of schools are related to the decreasing number of people attending churches within Christian traditions.

Theological schools are also changing in their educational delivery as seminaries seek to adapt their educational models in response to the needs of the church. Schools' responses during the global pandemic of 2020 represent some of the most dramatic changes. Prior to the pandemic about two-thirds of ATS schools offered courses online. During the COVID outbreak, all schools went to some form of remote delivery because of social distancing. In 2022, as faculty and students returned to campuses, seminaries continued to offer courses online. Among the accredited schools in the Commission on Accrediting of ATS, almost 93 percent of schools are now approved for some form of distance learning, and 86 percent are approved for comprehensive distance education, i.e., they are certified to offer degrees completely online.

Theological schools are also changing in terms of the students whom they serve. Through most of the twentieth century, students in theological schools were predominantly white, Euro-American. Since the early 1990s until the early 2020s, racial/ethnic and visa students have grown from 25 percent of all ATS students to 45 percent. In that time, white students are down 19 percent, students of Asian descent are up 122 percent, Hispanic Latine students are up 243 percent, Native/Indigenous students are up 69 percent, and visa students are up 38 percent.

In sum, these changes add up to tangible ways that theological schools are adapting, reflecting the changing landscape of US Christianity. The narratives of both Bexley Hall and Seabury-Western Theological Seminaries, who later became the Bexley Hall Seabury Western Seminary Federation, have elements of all these tectonic shifts named above. In this way, Bexley Seabury is a living example of an adaptive Mainline school in the twenty-first century.

What is not seen in these dramatic transformations are the countless acts of integrity. In the spring of 2008, before the great recession and market collapse, in a board meeting of a small Episcopal seminary in Evanston, Illinois, the trustees voted to declare financial exigency and terminate the faculty. On the surface, this would sound like another institution falling victim to the winds of change in higher education. What this news headline would not capture was the fact that this decision, which Seabury-Western Theological Seminary made in 2008, was the beginning of a new chapter. Without that faithful decision, there would never have been a Bexley Seabury that is now property-free, offering formational programs and degrees online for the current and future leadership needs of The Episcopal Church. The headline would also miss a small action that was taken minutes before the declaration of exigency, in which the board voted to grant tenure and promotion to its first faculty person of color in the school's long history, a young scholar named Frank Yamada. For that decision, I remain grateful to the board and my faculty colleagues. This small act of faithfulness changed my life and was a critical step on my road to administrative leadership in theological schools.

Introduction

THE TIME FOR A new history of Bexley Hall and Seabury-Western is long, long overdue. The last history of Bexley Hall Seminary was written in 1974,[1] and the most recent published history of Seabury-Western Theological Seminary is from 1936.[2] Both histories were produced in the wake of substantive changes: the 1974 history of Bexley Hall came six years after its relocation to Rochester, New York, to join the Colgate Rochester Divinity School consortium. The 1936 history of Seabury-Western came three years after the merger of Western Seminary and Bishop Seabury Divinity School in 1933 and the opening of the new Evanston campus.

It would be a bit of an understatement to say that much has transpired in the lives of Bexley Hall and Seabury-Western since 1974 and 1936, respectively. Yet in addition to these changes that have taken place in these two institutions, there have been tremendous changes in The Episcopal Church, religious identity and expression in North America, and in higher education. This will be a key theme in this history of Bexley Seabury Seminary Federation. Seminaries do not exist in historical vacuums, and the story of these two seminaries in many ways reflects, refracts, and exemplifies broader changes in The Episcopal Church, North American Christianity, and theological education. This bicentennial history of Bexley Hall Seabury-Western Seminary Federation comes after nearly fifteen years of transformative and wide-reaching changes

1. Spielmann, Bexley Hall, 150 Years.
2. McElwain, Norwood, and Grant, "Seabury Western Theological Seminary," 286–311.

Introduction

in the lives of both institutions, while The Episcopal Church itself has also undergone profound development during that same time period.

This history will examine the predecessor bodies to Bexley Hall Seabury Seminary Federation:

- Bexley Hall, part of the Protestant Theological Seminary of the Protestant Episcopal Church in the Diocese of Ohio, and located in Gambier, Ohio, from 1824–1968;
- Bishop Seabury Divinity School, part of a series of ecclesiastical and education institutions established in Faribault, Minnesota, in 1858;
- Western Seminary, founded in Chicago, Illinois, in 1883;
- Seabury-Western Theological Seminary, created by the merger of Western Seminary and Bishop Seabury Divinity School, with a campus in Evanston, Illinois, from 1933–2009;
- Bexley Hall's sojourn as a constituent member of the Colgate Rochester Divinity School (CRDS), later Colgate Rochester Crozier Divinity School (CRCDS), from 1968–1998;
- Bexley Hall's separation from CRCDS and reestablishment as a separate seminary, with campuses in Rochester, New York, and Columbus, Ohio, providing theological education in partnership with CRCDS and Trinity Lutheran Seminary, from 1998–2012;
- Seabury-Western's suspension of its master of divinity program, selling of its campus in Evanston to Northwestern University, and transformation into SeaburyNext from 2009–2012, located at the Churchwide Center of the Evangelical Lutheran Church in America in Chicago, Illinois;
- the federation of Bexley Hall and Seabury-Western as Bexley Hall Seabury-Western Seminary Federation, from 2012 to the present, relocated in 2016 to Chicago Theological Seminary in the Hyde Park region of Chicago.

INTRODUCTION

That is no fewer than eight different predecessor bodies involving seven different campus locations across two hundred years of operation.

At first, this might seem like a daunting task. Yet this history will not be an unfolding of a litany of changes, calamities, and deus ex machina deliverances. Nor will it be a triumphalist history about how what has not killed one only makes one stronger—though there are elements of both these literary devices and more in the backstory of Bexley Hall and Seabury-Western. Rather, we will look at some important themes that shape the narrative as it unfolds as organizing principles.

One of these themes involves taking into account the broader history of theological education to provide perspective.[3] As we look at the history of these seminaries, we run the risk of a pitfall all too prevalent in looking at the past: the danger of projecting a particular understanding or conception into the past, or presuming that a particular incarnation of an ecclesial institution is somehow normative. All elements of American Christianity have gone through profound development and change. Parishes, General Convention, bishops, vestries—all did not look or function the same way in the 1800s as they do now. Bishops used to have full-time day jobs as college presidents or rectors; vestries once were not elected by the parish as a whole; parishes used to be funded solely through pew sales and/or rentals. All elements of the church have gone through processes of change and development. Theological education and seminaries are no different.

The Bexley Hall of 1824 is different from the Bexley Hall of 1874 and 1924 and 1944 and 1974. The Seabury-Western of the 1990s was very different from that of the 1950s and 1930s, let alone the realities of its pre-merger predecessors.

Looking at the broader historical backdrop of theological education in the United States provides crucial context. First

---

3. The main history of theological education in the United States is Glenn Miller's *Piety and Intellect: The Aims and Purposes of Antebeullum Theological Education* and *Piety and Profession: American Protestant Theological Education, 1870–1970*.

INTRODUCTION

off: Bexley Seabury Seminary still exists and functions as a degree-granting institution, and continues to serve The Episcopal Church.[4] The history of theological education in the United States is littered with institutions that ceased to function, merged with other schools and effectively disappeared and were subsumed into those institutions, or continue to exist but no longer are degree-granting organizations.

Secondly: Bexley Seabury Seminary Federation reflects the ways in which theological education has developed and evolved over the past two hundred years in the United States. Bexley Hall looked different in 1824 because theological education looked very different; Bishop Seabury Divinity School looked different in the 1860s because theological education was different than it would be later. And yes, Bexley Hall and Seabury Western looked different in the 1970–1990 period because theological education has undergone profound change and development in the past fifty years: theological education is no longer primarily an overwhelmingly white, male, residential paradigm.

What were some of those changes and developments?

From 1820–1930, theological education evolved from what was in many ways a competency-based model focused on assisting students in mastering a body of doctrine and dogma. The Episcopal Church had established its Course of Ecclesiastical Studies, approved by General Convention, which listed what works were considered essential knowledge for persons preparing for ordained ministry. Seminary education involved assisting students in gaining proficiency in that learning. This was supplemented by particular emphases or interests of the schools themselves. For instance, Virginia Theological Seminary, with its low church, evangelical heritage, at one point required students to memorize the Thirty-Nine Articles of Religion of the Church. On the other hand, General Theological Seminary, with its high church, Anglo-Catholic

---

4. In discussing this history, I in no way intend any pejorative overtones in discussing schools that no longer exist or no longer function as degree granting institutions. Different schools made decisions based on their own contexts and spread over hundreds of years. The comparisons here are simply noting the broader historical reality of how different schools have evolved.

Introduction

milieu, included prominent Anglo-Catholic theologian Francis Hall's Dogmatic Theology in its curriculum. "Recitation" was the most common form of pedagogy, where students read essential texts, and the role of professors, more akin to a tutor, was to assist them in summarizing the essential elements of those texts. This is why editions of essential textbooks in the 1860–1950 period often had outlines at the head of each chapter, and short, one-sentence summaries of the points made in each paragraph in the margins. Theological education did not place much emphasis on preaching, pastoral theology, or what we would now call field education.

That is because of the competency-based component to theological education: most students did not attend seminary at all, and a significant portion of those who attended did not receive a degree, but would attend for a time to study what either they, their bishop, or their diocesan Board of Examining Chaplains thought they needed to study. Up until the 1920s, a sizable number of clergy in The Episcopal Church trained for ministry through a process of reading for orders and apprenticing with an experienced clergyperson, perhaps with a smattering of seminary courses. Even those who had received a seminary degree had received little formal training in preaching or pastoral care; it was expected this would be acquired through a curacy or other mentorship. Seminaries did not have much in the way of field education or practical training because it was not expected that this was their responsibility, and those preparing for ministry would be trained by others in these areas.

In addition, there was little distinction throughout the 1800s and well into the 1900s between "graduate" and "undergraduate" training; indeed, well into the 1950s, the foundational degree in theological education would continue not to be a graduate degree, but the bachelor of divinity. Faculty often did not have any graduate training of their own, or, if they did, perhaps a master of arts or bachelor of divinity. Seminary faculties were small, and, while there were what we might call "departments," seminary faculty overall were what we would consider generalists.

INTRODUCTION

Theological education in the 1820–1930 period also saw the emergence of two main models of theological schools: those that were attached in some way to a college or university, or else a standalone, independent institution. Bexley Hall Seabury-Western Seminary reflects both of these streams: for 144 years, Bexley Hall was the theological school of Kenyon College, while both Western Seminary and Bishop Seabury Divinity School were standalone, independent theological schools.

Through the 1920s, we see the beginnings of significant shifts that would set into motion massive changes in theological education. First and foremost is an increase in the professionalization of the ministry. These efforts are part of broader shifts in American society: prior to the 1900s, many teachers, attorneys, medical doctors, and nurses did not attend any formal training school. But we begin to see a push toward standards and professionalization in teaching, nursing, medicine, law, along with many other professions, including the ministry. We see the distinction made between graduate and undergraduate education, and the move toward the requirement of a bachelor's degree for seminary admissions. There is the corresponding professionalization of faculty, with expectations of graduate and later doctoral degrees, and the departmentalization of specially trained faculty teaching specific courses in their areas. It is with this move toward professionalization that seminaries place increased emphasis in other areas of training: more courses in pastoral theology, preaching, what we would call social ministry, and practical training / field education. These movements will crystalize in the 1930s with the formation of the American Association of Theological Schools (AATS), now known as the Association of Theological Schools. By the 1930s, a majority of clergy in The Episcopal Church will have attended seminary, and by the 1970s the overwhelming majority will attend seminary.

There is another crucial aspect of context that is essential in telling the story of Bexley Seabury Seminary Federation: theological education stands at a crucial nexus, reflecting two strands of development. Theological education is impacted by developments

INTRODUCTION

in higher education; as noted, much of what has been said about ministry can be said about law, teaching, medicine, social work, nursing, and many other professions. In addition, theological education is shaped by developments in North American Christianity and The Episcopal Church.

To put it another way: in the 1950s, the then-named American Association of Theological Schools commissioned a sweeping survey and report on the current state of theological education, enlisting one of the preeminent scholars of American religion, H. Richard Niebuhr, to serve as the chair of the task force to conduct the report. Niebuhr identified an important first principle for the survey, which is reflected in the title of the eventual report: *The Purpose of the Church and Its Ministry*.[5] Crucially, Niebuhr pointed out that seminaries, university divinity schools, and other forms of theological education do not exist for themselves. They are in the service of the advancement of the gospel as well as to particular denominations or ecclesiastical bodies. If the main purpose of theological education is to prepare persons for the ministry, then what is the ministry for which they are being prepared? What are the goals of the denominations in which they will eventually minister? Niebuhr penned a lengthy theological reflection and introduction to the commissioned survey, in which he states that engaging in an overview of education necessitates an examination of the broader landscape of Christianity. We must spend some time pondering "the purpose of the church, if a main goal of theological education is preparing people for ministry."[6]

Looking at the history of Bexley Seabury Seminary Federation is part of a broader reflection on the history and development of The Episcopal Church: these seminaries were not established, and did not make the decisions they did over the course of their lifetimes, in isolation. Rather than solely a history of Bexley Seabury Seminary Federation, this overview is, keeping with the spirit of Niebuhr's 1956 report, a reflection on the purposes of Bexley Seabury and its predecessor bodies, purposes in service

---

5. Niebuhr, *Purpose of the Church in Its Ministry*.
6. As quoted in Miller, *Piety and Profession*, 674.

INTRODUCTION

of the broader purpose of The Episcopal Church. Bexley Seabury Seminary Federation and its predecessor bodies were profoundly impacted by broader changes happening in The Episcopal Church outside of its own control, and both adapted to broader changes and developments in The Episcopal Church and North American Christianity.

It bears repeating: the history of Bexley Seabury Seminary Federation stands at the nexus of two poles of change, evolution, and development. It has been profoundly shaped by massive changes in how higher education has been understood over the past two hundred years. In addition, Bexley Seabury has also been impacted by broader changes and developments in The Episcopal Church and North American Christianity.

Appreciating these elements is simply crucial. It is crucial, in part, in reframing perceived or received narratives about Bexley Seabury and its predecessor bodies. Given these cycles of change and evolution, we need to be wary of presuming any particular incarnation as somehow "normative." To be sure, Bexley Hall had a long run—144 years!—in Gambier, Ohio, on the campus of Kenyon College. Likewise, Seabury-Western Theological Seminary can be considered to have entered a boomtime of growth in the 1950–1990 timeframe, as the student body and faculty grew in number. But should we consider either of these periods as definitive or somehow capturing an essential element of either body? Or do these particular time periods instead show how the seminaries were, in turn, reflecting and adapting to the current realities shaping higher education and The Episcopal Church?

Taking these aspects into account gives us a different perspective not only on the past, but on how we understand the present and the future. Ink has been spilled on Bexley Hall and/or Seabury-Western "closing" or "ceasing to exist." But that perpetuates taking any one perceived incarnation as normative. Bexley Hall ceased to function at various times in its history; in the mid-1870s, it had no faculty. During World War II, it relocated to Virginia Seminary. Even the official history of Western Seminary states at times it was

INTRODUCTION

"defunct" and had reached an "untenable nadir."[7] In the past twenty years, Bexley Hall and Seabury-Western underwent profound changes. Looking at the broader historical perspective, this should not be surprising or even unexpected – because higher education, The Episcopal Church, and North American Christianity have undergone profound changes in the past twenty years. Naturally the seminaries would as well. It is not that changes have occurred; in this overview, we will look at how Bexley Seabury adapted to those changes.

Thus a new history of Bexley Seabury is long overdue in order to look at its history against this backdrop of how higher education and The Episcopal Church have also changed and developed in the past two hundred years. The prior institutional histories were, by and large, overwhelmingly institutionally focused: so-and-so served as dean, these people were on the faculty, these alumni got elected bishop or were otherwise prominent, these were the financial challenges faced, here are the buildings that burned down. A major focus of this overview is to put significant events in a broader context.

A new history of Bexley Seabury is also long overdue because of the church's commitment to the full inclusion of all persons. Bexley Seabury's predecessor bodies were steeped in maleness and whiteness for the overwhelming majority of its existence. Bexley Seabury stands alongside the broader Episcopal Church in this, to be sure, but simply because it reflected its era does not mean we do not need to examine how Bexley Seabury reflected systemic racism, sexism, and marginalization of LGBTQIA+ persons. An examination of the seminary's complicity in these areas also necessitates the recovery of persons and narratives specifically marginalized and erased. For instance, the official sesquicentennial history of Bexley Hall notes that the seminary graduated its first African American student in 1859—this would make it the first Episcopal seminary to do so, yet the official history does not mention this person's name. Likewise, when James Lloyd Breck established the Bishop Seabury Divinity School, it was as part of a broader

---

7. Spielmann, *Bexley Hall, 150 Years*, 75–76.

INTRODUCTION

suite of educational institutions and organizations—including a school for Native Americans. The academies Breck established for primary education were only for white children of European descent; it would have been unthinkable for any Native Americans to have attended those schools. Rather, the school for Native Americans was specifically part of the broader effort to "civilize" Native Americans through education, and, perhaps not coincidentally, at the first sign of financial challenges was closed in order to focus on the education of white children in the academies and white seminarians preparing for ministry. Even as late as the early 1990s, there was not a single female tenure-track faculty member on the Seabury-Western faculty. A new history of Bexley Seabury must take into account how it has historically been centered in structures of white male supremacy.

As Bexley Seabury stands on the precipice of its third century, we now go back to the beginning, with the establishment of the Protestant Theological Seminary in the state of Ohio in 1824.

CHAPTER 1

Beginnings
Bexley Hall, 1824–1968

THE HISTORY OF BEXLEY Hall Seminary for its first fifty years is in many ways linked with the personalities of the first two bishops of the Episcopal Diocese of Ohio: Philander Chase (bishop from 1818 to 1831) and Charles McIlvaine (bishop from 1832 to 1873). Following the death of Bishop McIlvaine, the arc of the seminary's history from 1873 to 1968 revolved around the relationship between the seminary and Kenyon College and reflected substantive changes in both higher education in the United States and The Episcopal Church, leading to Bexley Hall leaving Gambier and become part of the Colgate Rochester Divinity School.

Bishop Chase and the Founding of the Theological Seminary of the Protestant Episcopal Church in the State of Ohio

Chase's personal life and ministry reflect in many ways the state of The Episcopal Church at the time. Born in New Hampshire, he was raised in the Congregational Church (the historic and predominant denomination in the state, and which remained the state-supported established church until 1817) and attended Dartmouth College. While at Dartmouth, he discovered The Episcopal Church through a copy of the *Book of Common Prayer* in the college library. This itself reflects the tenuous state of Anglicanism in New England after the Revolution. When Chase was born in 1775, there was not a single functioning Anglican parish in the state of New Hampshire. By the time he left home to attend Dartmouth, there was one functioning parish. As a result of his exposure to The Episcopal Church, he sought ordination and had to travel all the way to Albany to find a parish with a rector able to mentor him as he read for Holy Orders. Chase would become active in frontier and missionary work. Ordained by Bishop Samuel Provoost in the Diocese of New York, he first served in frontier parishes in western New York. In 1803 he became the first Protestant minister in the newly acquired territory of Louisiana, as rector of newly established Christ Church, New Orleans. After a sojourn in Hartford, Connecticut, he embarked again to the frontier, arriving in Ohio 1817 to serve as rector of a cluster of parishes in and around Columbus. In 1818 he was elected bishop by the handful of Episcopalians present in the state—only four clergypersons were resident in the state, and ten congregations had been gathered.

In Chase's very first Convention address in 1819 he called for the establishment of a "college" and had already founded Worthington Academy.[1] Chase became increasingly convinced of the need for a school on the frontier to provide for clergy, which were sorely needed—by 1823, the number of resident clergy in the Diocese of Ohio had increased from four all the way to . . . six. Meanwhile, between 1810 and 1820, the population of the state had more than doubled, and would nearly double again between 1820 and 1830. Chase could clearly see The Episcopal Church, already reduced in size due to the upheavals of the American Revolution, was falling

---

1. As we consider the early history of Bexley Hall, it is important to keep in mind the incredible fluidity in how educational terms were used, well into the 1870s and 1880s. There often were not clear boundaries between "high school" and "college," and it was common for college courses to be a mixture of what we would now consider high school and baccalaureate training—just it was common in what we would now call professional or graduate training to have a mixture of general education "college" courses alongside specialized training courses. The terms "college" and "seminary" at times referred to undergraduate institutions, and sometimes to what we would now call high school or secondary schools.

behind in the mission field on the frontier. In his 1823 address, Chase lamented, "With anguish of heart inexpressible, I have been forced to see the field of God's husbandry lie waste for the want of laborers."[2] In October of 1823, Chase sailed for England on a fundraising effort.

This effort was not without controversy. The bishops of The Episcopal Church were almost universally opposed to Chase's effort; instead, they sought to focus support on the newly created General Theological Seminary. A special General Convention was called in 1821, in large part to determine how best to apportion a significant bequest the church received. The Special General Convention created The General Theological Seminary and established the first incarnation of what would eventually become the Domestic and Foreign Missionary Society of The Protestant Episcopal Church. The General Theological Seminary, as its name indicated, was intended to be the seminary for The Episcopal Church as a whole, and it was established by General Convention with significant involvement of the Convention enshrined in its governance.[3] John Henry Hobart (bishop of New York, 1811–1830) advocated strongly for the newly established seminary to be located in his diocese and did his best to undermine Chase's fundraising efforts, seeing this as a direct challenge. Hobart, for instance, brought up the matter that Chase was an enslaver, having purchased a slave while rector in New Orleans, in order to tarnish Chase in the eyes of prominent evangelical members of the Church of England, who were largely opposed to slavery and the slave trade. Chase, in his defense, would in turn argue that he had emancipated the person he had enslaved.

The truth around his history as an enslaver is more complex than Chase's defense. When he arrived in New Orleans, Chase notes in his memoirs his need for domestic help: his wife struggled with illness, and he himself was not only serving a congregation

2. As quoted in Spielmann, *Bexley Hall, 150 Years*, 9.
3. General Convention would have a role in electing trustees to General, and the House of Bishops at times functioned as a kind of board of visitors providing oversight.

but also running a small school. There were no domestic servants available to employ for household help, so, as he recounts it, Chase reluctantly acquired an enslaved person: "In this undertaking the greatest difficulty that presented itself was the want of domestic servants. Where all are owners of slaves, no man can keep house without them. He must own them himself, or hire those belonging to others. No one would hire out good servants . . . . To borrow money and purchase was the only way left, except to give up and quit the country."[4]

Yet after three months, the person he enslaved, a man only referred to as Jack, escaped from Chase's enslavement. In his autobiography, Chase seethes with resentment at this, laying the sin entirely on Jack, and claims that he is the victim: "The writer [i.e., Chase] at that time thought it peculiarly unfortunate, hard pressed as he was, on all hands, and do his duty in that expensive place, to be so deceived by a slave."[5] Yet Chase also claims to have had a change of heart, and to come to oppose slavery as a sin. He notes that "mature reflection on the evils of slavery would heal the wound [of Jack's escape]."[6] Yet there is reason to doubt the depth of Chase's claim to have recognized the "evils" of slavery. Years later, Jack would be captured, and Chase, as his enslaver, was notified. Chase emancipated Jack rather than ask for compensation or continue his enslavement—yet he does so solely based on how others would think of him. He writes that "if his [that is, Chase][7] master were to reclaim and sell him [Jack] for money, his [Chase's] whole diocese would attribute it to a principle of covetousness, the great idol which at the present day all are so much inclined to worship, and thus his usefulness in Ohio would be destroyed forever."[8] In his own memoirs Chase shows little regard for Jack and only frees him so people wouldn't think he was greedy or overly concerned with money and thus think less of him. Chase's efforts at the time

---

4. Chase, *Reminiscences*, 74.
5. Chase, *Reminiscences*, 75.
6. Chase, *Reminiscences*, 75.
7. Chase routinely writes in the third person in his autobiography.
8. Chase, *Reminiscences*, 161.

to portray himself as a reluctant enslaver who had a change of heart regarding the evils of slavery seemed to assuage any concerns the predominantly anti-slavery evangelical movement in England might have had. Apart from Hobart's campaign against Chase, Presiding Bishop William White was also not supportive of Chase's fundraising tour, though, unlike Hobart, he did nothing directly to impede or hinder Chase's efforts.

Chase's fundraising tour was a success, resulting in pledges of up to thirty thousand dollars, equivalent to close to one million dollars, adjusted for inflation. However, having become the dog who caught the car, Chase and the diocesan Convention now had to decide what kind of institution to establish. In 1824 the institution was chartered as "the Theological Seminary of the Protestant Episcopal Church in the state of Ohio." Yet we need to keep in mind the varying and changing understandings of what a "seminary" meant, with the term still being used at the time to describe some schools that we would now consider to be a primary and/or secondary school.[9] Through discussions with the diocesan Convention and clergy and lay leaders, Chase eventually came around to the concept of an institution that would train clergy, to be sure, but also provide for other professions needed for the rapidly growing and expanding frontier. Chase was also adamant that the institution be founded in a rural location in the countryside, which was a healthier place to be, both physically (given bouts of yellow fever and other illnesses that were rampant in urban areas) and morally (with the temptations toward drink and vice perceived as prevalent in cities). He thus chose a rural region of the state, choosing to name the town established after one benefactor, Lord Gambier, and to name the college after another, Lord Kenyon. Later, when a dedicated seminary building would be constructed, it would be named after a third benefactor, Lord Bexley. The focus in the first several years was on gathering faculty and students. By 1830 there were roughly thirty students and two to three faculty members,

---

9. We still see an example of this with Friends Seminary, which is a Quaker K-12 school in New York City founded just before Kenyon College/Bexley Hall.

providing a general education program. As Spielmann notes in his history, "The Theological Seminary's first accomplishment was the building of Kenyon College."[10] While a handful of students were ordained who had attended, it is likely they attended the college's course of study, supplemented by directed study and reading for orders with Bishop Chase.

Any further efforts Chase might have in shaping the institution's development were cut short through the conflict surrounding his oversight of the seminary and diocese. Essentially, the small faculty present rebelled against Chase's complete control and oversight of the school, protesting that the faculty and board of trustees had little say in pretty much anything. Chase, in turn, argued that he was only following the current charter and constitution of the school which the diocesan convention had approved. The faculty would appeal to the Diocesan Convention of the Diocese of Ohio, which sided with them against the bishop. Chase then resigned as president of the school and as bishop of Ohio, moved to Illinois, where he was eventually elected the first bishop of Illinois, and started Jubilee College, another school for training of ministers and other professionals.

Bishop McIlvaine and the Growth of Bexley Hall and Kenyon College

Though Chase is remembered as the founder, it was Bishop Charles Pettit McIlvaine who had a greater role in shaping the development of Bexley Hall and Kenyon College. Part of this was due to the extraordinary length of his time as bishop—forty-one years!—and partly due to McIlvaine's force of personality, network of connections, and commitment to the evangelical wing of The Episcopal Church.

As McIlvaine himself noted, when he became bishop, there was not any kind of recognizable course of study for ministry preparation: "Prior to my coming to the Diocese . . . there had

---

10. Spielmann, *Bexley Hall, 150 Years*, 13–14.

been no course of study for theological students organized."[11] For several years in the early 1830s, no catalogs at all were published, and the few that were barely mentioned a program for theological education for ministry.

McIlvaine took a great interest in the development of what would become Bexley Hall. He initially chose to reside in Gambier itself, giving him day-to-day exposure to the governance of the school. In the 1830s, a number of significant actions by McIlvaine set Bexley Hall down a path that would shape the school's development for most of the 1800s. McIlvaine set about defining the relationship between what would become Kenyon and what would become Bexley Hall, between a college and a seminary. As noted in the introduction, and earlier in this chapter, terms like "college" and "seminary" and "academy" functioned very differently in pre–Civil War American higher education. There was no agreed upon, standard definition of what any of the terms meant, let alone hard and fast distinctions between "undergraduate" and "graduate" education. The broader context of the development of theological education is crucial here: these kinds of definitions were starting to take shape. Andover Theological Seminary had been founded in 1807 as the first standalone, specifically dedicated seminary for preparation for ministry. McIlvaine's efforts in Gambier were profoundly shaped by the fact that he had, in fact, attended one of the few dedicated seminaries currently in existence, which was related to a college, and which had already established these distinctions: throughout the 1800s, Princeton Theological Seminary was enormously influential in shaping what seminaries would come to look like and how they would function in American higher education.[12]

McIlvaine proceeded in three important and significant areas. The first was in terms of curriculum. By 1835, there was a dedicated faculty and a dedicated curriculum focused specifically

---

11. McIlvaine's address to the 1842 Diocesan Convention, as quoted in Spielmann, *Bexley Hall, 150 Years*, 18.

12. See Miller, *Piety and Intellect*, ch. 6, for an overview of Princeton Theological Seminary's substantial role in shaping understandings of seminary education in the United States.

on theological education and preparation for ministry. There was a clear sense that students preparing for ministry were separate from the collegiate student body, with a dedicated Declaration to which all students studying for ministry were required to subscribe, kept in a separate, dedicated Matriculation Book which all students from 1836 and onward have signed in some form, and which is still kept in the Bexley Seabury Seminary Federation's archives. There was a clear separation between collegiate and seminary education, faculty, curriculum, and student body.

Secondly, McIlvaine worked to define the structure and governance of the entity that operated a number of bodies under the umbrella legal incorporation of "The Theological Seminary of the Protestant Episcopal Church in the state of Ohio."[13] From 1838 to 1840, a number of decisions were taken clarifying matters of governance and the relationship of the college and the seminary. In 1839, in his address to the Diocesan Convention, McIlvaine spoke of Kenyon College as "an institution having no incorporation, no property, no trustees, no faculty except as a part and parcel of the Theological Seminary." In a speech given at the dedication of the cornerstone of Bexley Hall (and later printed and published as a pamphlet), McIlvaine spoke of the college as an "annex" and a "branch" of the seminary.[14] Several constitution changes were made in 1838–1839, approved by the Convention of the Diocese of Ohio, and confirmed by the House of Bishops (this was to fulfill a provision contained in the original constitution of the school, and later removed). There was a separation of the college and seminary faculty, with the designated college faculty certifying and awarding collegiate degrees, and the seminary faculty certifying and awarding theological degrees. Each had its own president, with the bishop of Ohio as president of the seminary by virtue of office. The bishop likewise had the sole authority to nominate the president of Kenyon College. McIlvaine also curtailed any efforts by the faculty

---

13. While we are focusing mostly on the college and seminary in this history, there was also a functioning academy / grammar school that operated throughout the 1800s and into the 1900s.

14. As quoted in Spielmann, *Bexley Hall, 150 Years*, 23.

to stage any sort of coup as attempted against Chase by including a provision that no faculty—not even the college president—could serve on the single board of trustees that governed the college and the seminary.

Having attended to curricular, faculty, and governance matters, McIlvaine was also central in giving the seminary its home and its name. Though not as celebrated as Chase's journey in 1824, McIlvaine went on his own fundraising tour of the United Kingdom in 1834–1835, returning with twelve thousand five hundred dollars (roughly three hundred seventy-five thousand dollars, adjusted for inflation) and nineteen hundred books specifically focused on theological education. In 1839, the cornerstone was laid for what was now called Bexley Hall. Bexley Hall, well into the 1900s, was the self-contained home for the seminary. The first floor contained classrooms, chapel, and library; the second floor had apartments and accommodations for the faculty; and student residences were on the third floor. Geographically, the landscape of McIlvaine's vision was taking shape. University Hall, which comprised the office and classrooms of the college, was at one end of the campus; Harcourt Parish, the worshiping community, was established in the center; and Bexley Hall was located at the other end of the path that connected the three buildings. College at one end, seminary at the other, with Harcourt Parish in between and serving as the spiritual center of the institutions.

It is under Bishop McIlvaine's tenure that Bexley Hall became the first Episcopal seminary to enroll an African American student. William Alston was born a free person in North Carolina and later attended Oberlin College. McIlvaine, who was active in antislavery and abolitionist causes, made Alston a postulant for Holy Orders, and in 1856 he was admitted as a student at Bexley Hall. William Jay, the son of John Jay, first attorney general of the United States, and himself an active Episcopalian and abolitionist, wrote to McIlvaine when he heard the news. Jay exulted in the news, and in thanking McIlvaine for admitting Alston expressed his gratitude that "the unholy prejudice of caste will receive no episcopal sanction in the diocese of Ohio." Jay contrasted McIlvaine's actions with the prevailing attitude among Episcopal bishops, noting that McIlvaine's advocacy in anti-slavery organizations "gives me peculiar opportunities of observing the disastrous influence exercised over not a few of them [bishops of The Episcopal Church] . . . by a large portion of the American Church in relation to caste and slavery." Jay also castigated the system of Episcopal seminary education. He recounts to McIlvaine the story of an African American who had completed part of a course of medical study by directed reading and correspondence in a local College of Physicians, who, when he showed up in person to complete his schooling, was denied attendance at lectures when they saw that he was not white. Jay then wrote, "But who can condemn those Doctors, when the Rt. Rev. and Rev. Mr. officers of the Theological Seminary[15] have previously refused to teach a man of unimpeachable character and literary attainments to heal those diseases of the Soul, because his skin was darker than their own?"[16] Jay concludes his letter by offering to completely finance Alston's education. Alston graduated in 1859 and was ordained to the transitional diaconate by Bishop McIlvaine. In 1860 he was ordained to the priesthood by Bishop Horatio Potter of the Diocese of New York. After serving for a short term at the historically African American parish of St. Philip's in Manhattan, in 1863 he was called as the third rector of St. Thomas African Episcopal Church in Philadelphia.[17]

Yet despite graduating the first African American with a bachelor of divinity degree, Bexley Hall would continue for decades to be entirely white and would not enroll additional African American students until the 1960s. Kenyon College would not enroll its first African American undergraduate students until 1952.

---

15. Jay is almost certainly referring to General Seminary and its decision to refuse admission to Alexander Crummell in the 1840s. "The Theological Seminary" was a common shorthand for General Seminary at the time, and Jay was one of the most prominent abolitionists in New York state.

16. Jay, "Letter to C.P. McIlvaine."

17. For more on Alston, see Bragg, *History of the Afro-American Group*,197–99. See also Bass, *Standing Against the Whirlwind*, 154; and Smith, *Bishop McIlvaine, Slavery, Britain*, 53.

BEGINNINGS

McIlvaine resided in Gambier for a number of years before eventually relocating to Cincinnati, but even after moving he continued to exercise considerable influence over Kenyon College and Bexley Hall. McIlvaine was one of the most well-known bishops in The Episcopal Church and one of the leaders of the evangelical wing of The Episcopal Church in the 1800s.[18] At its peak, perhaps 35–40 percent of Episcopal bishops prior to the Civil War identified with the evangelical wing of the church. McIlvaine railed against the Oxford Movement, condemned the *Tracts for the Times*, and was suspicious of "Romanizing" influences at General Seminary. McIlvaine linked Bexley Hall closely with the evangelical wing of The Episcopal Church. Throughout his forty years as bishop nearly half the students would be from the Diocese of Ohio, with other students predominantly coming from other prominent evangelical Episcopal dioceses. The seminary would see a boom in enrollment during the Civil War: Virginia Seminary, the other prominent evangelical seminary, was occupied by Union troops during the conflict. Some Northern evangelicals, unable to attend Virginia, attended Bexley instead—enrollment swelled from twenty-seven students in 1861 to thirty-nine in 1862. William Bodine, an alumnus of Bexley Hall and later president of Kenyon College, acknowledged this in his own writings, noting, "But for the Civil War . . . I should have gone, for my theological training, to Alexandria." When Virginia Seminary resumed operations, attendance quickly reverted to its antebellum pattern, with fourteen students enrolled at Bexley in 1866.

18. McIlvaine was influential and well-connected: his father was a US senator, and he variously served as a professor at West Point and chaplain to the US Senate as well as engaged with a number of abolitionist and anti-slavery organizations. Later he would be dispatched on a covert diplomatic mission by President Lincoln to try to use his ecclesial connections to lobby Great Britain to not extend diplomatic recognition to the Confederate States of America. Coincidentally, prominent Episcopalian Secretary of the Treasury Salmon P. Chase, Philander Chase's nephew, would be a go-between in negotiating this mission with McIlvaine and Lincoln. He would die in Florence, Italy, while on a European trip, and on the return journey home his body lay in state in Westminster Abbey for four days. He is the only American to receive this honor, and a plaque was erected in commemoration in Westminster Abbey.

McIlvaine's affiliation with the evangelical wing of the church would impact Bexley's fortunes. The evangelical party would see a remarkable decline in the post–Civil War period. Part of this decline would be due to fallout from the schism of the Reformed Episcopal Church in 1873, when George Cummins, assistant bishop of the Diocese of Kentucky, would form a separate denomination that rejected the influence of the Oxford Movement and Anglo-Catholicism and placed more emphasis on evangelical belief and practice. We can see this fallout at Bexley Hall as well. Charles Edward Cheney, a priest in the Diocese of Chicago, refused to include the word "regenerate" in the baptismal rite of the *Book of Common Prayer*. This had become a bit of a cause célèbre among evangelicals in the United Kingdom and in the United States, as a reaction against an Anglo-Catholic emphasis on the efficacy of the sacraments as a means of grace over and against individual conversion and experience of sanctifying grace. Cheney would later be deposed from the ministry by the bishop of Chicago, join Cummins's movement, and eventually become the second bishop in the Reformed Episcopal Church. The faculty at Bexley Hall, reflecting their strong roots in the evangelical wing of The Episcopal Church, sided with Edward Cheney, signing a petition calling for his reinstatement, for which they were censured by the board of trustees. In response to this censure, by the summer of 1873, all of the seminary faculty had resigned and left for other positions within the Church. By the fall of 1873, Bishop McIlvaine had died, and the seminary had no students enrolled and no active faculty for the 1873–1874 academic year.

From Civil War to World War II: The Long Beginning of the End of Bexley in Gambier

With the death of Bishop McIlvaine, long term trends were set in motion that would eventually result in the separation of Bexley Hall from Kenyon College and its relocation to Rochester. Two of the most important developments involve the Diocese of Ohio and Kenyon College.

Beginnings

The Diocese of Ohio, after the death of Bishop McIlvaine, never had the same level of hands-on involvement with Kenyon and Bexley. Even while Bishop McIlvaine moved to Cincinnati and no longer resided in Gambier, he still served under the governance established in the 1830s: he was president of the seminary and had sole right to appoint the president of Kenyon College. Bishop Bedell, his successor, relocated to Cleveland and took a much more hands-off approach to the seminary. This was, in part, likely due to the increasing complications that came with running a diocese in the 1870s and 1880s as opposed to the 1840s and 1850s: many bishops prior to the Civil War were not stipendiary and had other positions. Prior to the Civil War, much of the ministry of the church was done by voluntary associations. Independent organizations, funded through donations and dues, focused around specific causes and engaged in education, domestic and missionary efforts, and other initiatives. After the Civil War, the growth of the church and the growth of dioceses themselves necessitated that bishops had more duties and responsibilities, alongside the voluntary associations, which also went through processes of change and development.

In the 1880s, Bishop Bedell and the diocesan Convention instituted changes to governance that would have long-lasting implications. Under the previous Constitution, the bishop had served as what was called a "Prudential Committee." In between meetings of the board of trustees, the bishop alone served as an Executive Committee, able to make decisions on behalf of the board. This was replaced with an Executive Committee, consisting of trustees (along with the bishop of Ohio). A task force was then established to review the constitution and governance, which resulted in significant changes in the new constitution approved in 1892. While it was still chartered under the name "Protestant Theological Seminary of the Protestant Episcopal Church in the Diocese of Ohio" in order to grant degrees, its legal and corporate name for doing business was changed to Kenyon College. Whereas McIlvaine has previously spoken of the college as an "annex" to the seminary, the new constitution clearly defined a single institution with three departments. The single institution was Kenyon College, which had three departments: an undergraduate college (Kenyon), a theological seminary (Bexley Hall), and a preparatory secondary school (then called Kenyon Military Academy). All three departments were placed under the authority of a single board of trustees and a single president (previously the bishop of Ohio served as president of the seminary and chair of the board), who was no longer nominated by the bishop but chosen by the board. All property, funds, and endowments were under the control and authority of the board of trustees.[19]

The constitutional changes approved in 1892 removed the bishop, Diocese of Ohio, and The Episcopal Church from having any direct authority over the college and seminary. A contrast may be drawn with the University of the South, where the founding dioceses still comprise the board of trustees, while ceding day-to-day authority to a board of regents, which has resulted in significant involvement of sponsoring dioceses and The Episcopal Church with the University of the South to this day. These decisions made in the 1890s, removing the involvement of The Episcopal Church in the governance of Kenyon College, set in motion the eventual disengagement of Kenyon from any Episcopal moorings and the eventual separation of Bexley Hall.

The decisions in the 1892 constitution, in turn, reinforced tensions between the college and the seminary. Both were facing serious challenges as the 1800s turned to the 1900s, with the college and the seminary struggling for students and struggling financially. There began to be an increasing sense on the board that one of the reasons for Kenyon's struggle to recruit students was its church connections. In turn, the situation in Gambier reflects broader trends in higher education, with a number of colleges in the 1860–1920 period severing or reducing their ties to denominations, and the percentage of colleges with clergy serving as president dropped dramatically during this period. The actions taken to redefine the relationship between Kenyon and Bexley Hall, and

19. As outlined in the preface to the 1892–1893 catalogue, Kenyon College, "Catalogue 1892–1893," 5–6.

to reevaluate ecclesial connections, would be played out in a similar way in a number of colleges, universities, and seminaries as the 1800s turned to the 1900s.

Matters would come to a head in a series of crises in the 1920s. In the early 1900s there was continued decline at Bexley Hall, with perhaps twelve to fifteen students enrolled, and 75–80 percent of those from the Diocese of Ohio and Southern Ohio. The year 1921 saw only two students listed as completing studies, one with a "Certificate of Graduation" and one with the bachelor of divinity. With the hiring of Samuel Mercer as dean, the seminary saw a revival in fortunes, with an increase in enrollment. Dean Mercer was involved in two major initiatives that further shaped the long-term development of Bexley.

The first was that he proposed limited autonomy and oversight be given to Bexley Hall, with a separate board of visitors appointed by the board of trustees, and with its own budgetary oversight. The argument for this autonomy was so that Bexley Hall could focus on strengthening ties with The Episcopal Church, in order to raise funds and recruit students, at a time when the college was choosing to de-emphasize these connections. This was rejected by the Kenyon president and board of trustees, which chose to retain complete control over the seminary's governance and finances.

Yet the seminary saw a revival in its fortunes in the midst of these developments: the number of students increased. This was, in part, due to longer-term trends in theological education. The 1920s saw the beginning of a significant shift from the older, apprenticeship-based, reading for orders model, and we see increased numbers of Episcopal clergy now attending seminaries. Between 1920 and 1926, the student body grew from twelve to fifteen residential students to nearly thirty residential students. This revival in fortunes precipitated the next crisis that would fundamentally shape Bexley's trajectory. Increasing numbers of students meant the need for more faculty, more staff, and more resources in terms of housing. A major fundraising appeal for the seminary took place from 1925 to 1926 and was successful: nearly three hundred thousand dollars was raised through Episcopal Church networks for Bexley Hall (the rough equivalent of four million dollars adjusted for inflation). However, under the 1892 constitution, the Kenyon board of trustees had sole authority over any funds or endowments raised. Of the three hundred thousand dollars raised specifically for Bexley Hall, ninety-two thousand dollars was taken and placed into the Kenyon endowment to cover past and future deficits the seminary might incur. Subsequently, since it had raised so much, the Kenyon board of trustees ended its practice of providing funding for Bexley Hall from the draw on its own endowment. And, finally, since the seminary had raised a significant amount, Kenyon accordingly increased the amount it charged Bexley for administration, support services, and oversight. The result, as the dean of Bexley Hall noted in 1927, was that despite having raised such a significant amount, at the end of a successful capital campaign, the seminary was still running a deficit, and the appropriation of funds designated for the seminary by the college for its own endowment damaged relationships with Episcopal Church donors. The dean resigned in protest, and the relationship with the college never really recovered.

With the Great Depression, the 1930s saw additional financial pressures. One of the seminary faculty noted in his diary that Kenyon delayed repairs to the furnace in the seminary building, which for a time necessitated holding classes in the Common Room at Bexley Hall, which had a fireplace, since the classrooms were too cold to occupy. The late 1930s saw the first efforts at Kenyon to shut down Bexley Hall. Kenyon was running a deficit in the equivalent of over a hundred thousand dollars in current funds. A special task force was appointed, which recommended a series of options, including closing the seminary or having it cease to become a degree-granting institution of its own and instead offer the bachelor of divinity in partnership with another seminary. After fierce lobbying from the Dioceses of Ohio and Southern Ohio, the decision was made to keep the seminary functioning in its current status.

BEGINNINGS

These conversations, however, would soon be cut short, as World War II broke out, upending higher education and theological education. Massive resources were required for training an officer corps. Bexley Hall relocated to the campus of Virginia Theological Seminary from 1942 to 1945, and its facilities were given over to officer candidate training programs as part of civilian mobilization.

The Road to Relocation to Rochester, 1945–1968

After the conclusion of World War II, the path was set in place for Bexley Hall's eventual separation from Kenyon College. But paradoxically, this separation had nothing to do with the enrollment or financial struggles that marked the seminary's history. In the 1950s, enrollment boomed, averaging nearly forty-five students a year, and the finances improved accordingly. Bexley Hall relocated not because it was struggling, but because of broader trends over which it had no control, trends in both higher education and in The Episcopal Church.

The relationship between Kenyon and Bexley was profoundly shaped by changes in American higher education in the postwar period. Due to a number of shifts—the GI Bill making college affordable for millions of veterans, growing numbers of women attending college, the increasing professionalization of a number of vocations requiring undergraduate degrees, the growth of the middle class—the number of persons attending college boomed during the 1950s and 1960s. It is the increasing numbers of women attending college that directly impacted the Bexley and Kenyon relationship. Kenyon was still struggling financially, posting regular deficits into the 1960s. A report commissioned by the college determined it would need roughly fifteen hundred students (more than double its then-enrollment of seven hundred) to be on a sound economic footing. Admitting more male students would require lowering admissions standards, so the school decided to become a fully coeducational institution. The college needed more space for this increase in enrollment and wanted to place its focus on undergraduate education. We see this in the timing of Bexley's relocation. It is no coincidence that Bexley Hall left Kenyon in the spring of 1968, and the first women students arrived in the fall of 1969. The two conversations—the separation of Bexley from Kenyon and implementing a plan for coeducation—were inextricably linked and took place concurrently.[20] In addition, the 1950s and 1960s saw increasing secularization of higher education, and Kenyon, like many other colleges, was going through a process of further de-emphasizing its ecclesial and denominational background and heritage.

Bexley was also being shaped by changes in The Episcopal Church and in theological education. Bishop Chase had deliberately chosen to establish the college and seminary in a rural environment, which he deemed morally and physically healthier than being in the city. Yet by the 1950s and 1960s, Bexley's rural location had increasingly become a challenge, due to sweeping changes in society.

Practically, its location was a challenge to Bexley in responding to the reshaping of theological education in the postwar period. Through the first half of the twentieth century, theological education had shifted from its paradigm of focus on biblical languages, significant study of the Bible, and mastering a body of dogmatic or confessional knowledge toward adapting to the wave of professionalization and practical training. Field education and practical learning, which had been barely part of the curriculum prior to the 1920s, had become a significant emphasis. With the establishment of the American Association of Theological Schools in the 1930s, field education and practical training became a component of academic accreditation.[21] Bexley's rural location and lack of nearby parishes made it simply difficult to provide the necessary field education training, with students often fulfilling these obligations over the summer. A report issued in 1959 examining Bexley Hall, funded by the Lilly Endowment and chaired by the future Presiding Bishop Arthur Lichtenberg, bluntly stated that if the seminary

---

20. See Spielmann, *Bexley Hall, 150 Years*, 94–96.
21. See discussions in Miller, *Piety and Profession*, chs. 19 and 25.

were to be founded today, it would never be located in as remote an area as Gambier.²²

This was combined with an increasing emphasis on the need of The Episcopal Church to respond to massive shifts toward urbanization. By the post–World War II period, most Episcopal parishes were located in cities and suburbs. In terms of mission, cities were areas to which the church increasingly turned, reaching a peak at the 1967 General Convention. Presiding Bishop John Hines called for the establishment of a churchwide program to address urban issues, which became the General Convention Special Program, funded with three million dollars over the 1967–1970 triennium, equivalent to nearly twenty million dollars as adjusted for inflation. There was also the prevailing sentiment that The Episcopal Church had too many seminaries. In the days when travel had been more painstaking and difficult, it might have made sense to have more regional seminaries, but first the railroad and then air travel and the interstate highway system reshaped dynamics. The 1960s would see movements eventually leading to Philadelphia Divinity School merging with Episcopal Theological School in Cambridge, and Berkeley Divinity School affiliating with Yale Divinity School.

While these developments had been years in the making, when the separation came, it came relatively quickly. At the Opening of School ceremony in 1965, the Kenyon president, as part of his formal remarks, stated that the coming academic year "may be the year of decision" for the relationship between Kenyon and Bexley. A flurry of meetings took place over the 1965–1966 academic year, with a number of options discussed, including closing, merging, or relocating the seminary. In the spring of 1966, the Kenyon board of trustees voted to create an independent board of trustees for Bexley Hall, charged with deciding the future of the seminary. The Kenyon board further voted that a plan for the seminary had to be presented by February of 1967, and the seminary would need to cease to be part of Kenyon by June of 1967.

---

22. As summarized in Spielmann, *Bexley Hall, 150 Years*, 87.

Negotiations concerning financial, property, and legal matters, as is often the case, at times became bitter and contentious. The constitution that was reworked in the 1890s vested all assets in Kenyon, so the decision was made that there would be no compensation given to Bexley for any of the seminary buildings, even those that had been built using funds donated by The Episcopal Church (though Kenyon also assumed any existing mortgage liabilities). Endowment funds were surveyed, and only those clearly and specifically marked for theological education for ministry were designated for Bexley. As Richard Spielmann, who was on the Bexley Hall faculty at the time, glumly noted: "The Committee [set up to divide property and endowments] decided all gray areas went to Kenyon."[23]

While Bexley was negotiating the terms of its separation with Kenyon, it also needed to find a new home. There were two particular elements that shaped the decision of where Bexley Hall should relocate. The first was a commitment to be part of an urban environment, reflecting issues that had been raised for decades around its rural location. The second was a commitment to be part of a broader ecumenical partnership. In addition to a shift toward the cities, the 1960s also saw a tremendous flowering of ecumenical dialogues and partnerships. The Consultation on Church Union (COCU) was established in 1962 with The Episcopal Church as a founding member, seeking closer partnership among a number of historic Protestant denominations. Anglican–Roman Catholic and Anglican–Eastern Orthodox Dialogues were established, both internationally through the Anglican Communion and locally in the United States.

The committee tasked with determining the future of Bexley Hall initially presented four options, two Episcopal and two non-Episcopal. One Episcopal option was Philadelphia Divinity School, which was located in an urban environment and was another small, struggling Episcopal seminary looking toward merger; the other was the Church Divinity School of the Pacific (CDSP), located in an urban setting (Berkeley, California) and part of the newly

---

23. Spielmann, *Bexley Hall, 150 Years*, 68.

created ecumenical consortium, the Graduate Theological Union. The two non-Episcopal options were urban, intentionally ecumenically minded seminaries: Eden Seminary in St. Louis, Missouri, and Colgate Rochester Divinity School (CRDS) in Rochester, New York. The list of four would be narrowed to CDSP and CRDS, and eventually CRDS would be chosen. The minutes of the committee list the reasons for their choice:

> The committee by a majority vote favored Colgate Rochester. In more specific terms, Colgate Rochester was judged . . . to have a close and productive relationship with a university of growing prominence [the University of Rochester], to offer immediate ecumenical associations and the rather tangible prospect of a close association with the Roman Catholic seminary (St. Bernard's), to be located in an adequately large city offering the normal variety of urban activities and problems, and to be capable of easily and successfully accommodating Bexley Hall's faculty and students, and finally to represent a geography remote enough from the seminary-saturated Atlantic Coast and yet close enough to secure Ohio interest and support.[24]

In the end, it was CRDS's relationship with St. Bernard's, and its geographic location allowing for continued relationships with Bexley's historic base in Ohio, that tipped the scales. The 1968 commencement was Bexley's last in Gambier. A relationship of 144 years had drawn to a close.

---

24. As quoted in Spielmann, *Bexley Hall, 150 Years*, 99–100.

CHAPTER 2

Beginnings

Bishop Seabury Divinity School, 1858–1933
Western Theological Seminary, 1883–1933
Formation of Seabury-Western Theological Seminary, 1933

WE NOW SHIFT TO the establishment and development of the two predecessor bodies of Seabury-Western Seminary: what eventually comes to be designated Bishop Seabury Divinity School, founded in Faribault, Minnesota, in 1858; and Western Seminary, founded in Chicago in 1883.

With the establishment of Bishop Seabury Divinity School, we will be able to see some parallels to the formation of Kenyon College and Bexley Hall a generation earlier. Both were founded on what was then the frontier, to provide contextual education and training for ministry on the frontier; and both were the product of a visionary founder succeeded by a second individual arguably more important long-term than the initial founder. On the other hand, as we look at the establishment of Western Seminary, we will see some different dynamics come into play: the formation of a regional, largely (but by no means entirely) diocesan training program, with analogs to Kentucky Theological Seminary and Berkeley Divinity School.

BEGINNINGS

Formation of the Bishop Seabury Mission

The analog to Bishop Philander Chase in the story of Bishop Seabury Divinity School is another person with an equally remarkable (and peripatetic) missionary career, James Lloyd Breck (1818–1876). Breck was educated at the Flushing Institute, a secondary school founded by the visionary nineteenth-century Episcopal Church leader William Augustus Muhlenberg. Muhlenberg would be an enormous influence on Breck, to the point that Breck would name one of his children after him. As has been noted by William Haugaard,[1] Breck's missionary efforts fall into roughly four different eras, each consisting of approximately eight to nine years. From 1841 to 1850 Breck was part of the group that founded Nashotah House. He moved to Minnesota and from 1850 to 1858 was engaged in missionary efforts among Native Americans; then from 1858 to 1867 he shifted his base of operations to Faribault, Minnesota, where he established what was called the Bishop Seabury Mission, an umbrella entity for a collection of schools and missionary efforts. In 1867 he resigned all of his positions in Faribault and relocated to California, where he founded two more schools and served as rector before his death in 1876 in Benicia, California.

Breck's efforts in establishing the Bishop Seabury Mission in 1858 are an outgrowth of his prior experiences at Nashotah House. Nashotah House was understood as much more than a place for training clergy. Nashotah was seen as a center of mission and missionary efforts, with a religious community gathered at the House sending missionaries into the surrounding area, to organize efforts among white settlers and for missionary efforts to Native Americans. Breck very consciously adapted his efforts in Faribault on the Nashotah model. He referred to both Nashotah House and the school for training persons for ministry in Minnesota as "schools for prophets," and likewise saw these efforts at establishing a series of schools as essential to larger missionary efforts. He later wrote, reflecting on his time in Minnesota, that

---

1. Haugaard, "Missionary Vision of James Lloyd Breck," 242.

the "plan for Evangelizing a country such as ours, or any heathen land, was inaugurated at Nashotah, because it was primitive and catholic. Under this system, Nashotah has sent forth one hundred Missionaries already, and caused the Church in Wisconsin to bud and blossom as the rose. This same system in Minnesota, was an offshoot from Nashotah."[2]

Breck's efforts in establishing a system of educational institutions in Faribault is also inextricably linked to his missionary efforts among Native Americans. Breck was a deacon when he helped establish Nashotah House in 1841; when time came for his ordination to the priesthood, he insisted it be in a church building that had been consecrated by a bishop. There were only two such buildings in Wisconsin at the time, one of them being the Church of the Holy Apostles in Oneida, Wisconsin, a mission church of the Oneida Nation.[3] Missionary Bishop Jackson Kemper ordained Breck to the priesthood, and after the ceremony Breck returned to Nashotah with three young Oneida to be educated, one of whom would eventually become the first Oneida ordained to the priesthood.

In 1850, Breck relocated to Minnesota, to a newer frontier, to continue missionary work. This would eventually lead to his efforts among the Lakota/Dakota and Ojibwe (who are nearly universally referred to in the white sources of the nineteenth century as Chippewa or Chippeway). Breck gathered a congregation in St. Paul, at that time a town of barely fifteen hundred people. A transformative meeting would occur in that mission church in 1851 when an Ottawa Indian named Enmegahbowh arrived to have his son educated in the small primary school Breck had also established.

---

2. As quoted in Haugaard, "Missionary Vision of James Lloyd Breck," 243–44.

3. Due to encroachment of white settlers, and abrogation of treaties by the state of New York, Oneida holdings in central New York had been reduced to a few dozen acres by the 1820s. This led a group of Oneida to move to Wisconsin, where they acquired millions of acres of land. To this day there are two recognized branches of the Oneida people, one in New York State and one in Wisconsin. See Wisconsin Department of Public Instruction, "Oneida Nation." https://dpi.wi.gov/amind/tribalnationswi/oneida, accessed 5/23/2024.

Enmegahbowh had spent some time in the Methodist Church before being introduced to the *Book of Common Prayer* by the Episcopal military chaplain at Fort Snelling, Minnesota. It would be Enmegahbowh who invited Breck to engage in missionary work in central Minnesota, and Bishop Kemper would give his consent for Breck to move to Gull Lake, near what is currently Brainerd, Minnesota, in 1852. For six years Breck ministered to Lakota/Dakota and Ojibwe based out of what was eventually named St. Columba Mission. Breck would withdraw from the mission and end his missionary efforts due to resistance from some of the local peoples. He recounts an incident when he had to barricade himself in a room and declared that he could not remain in St. Columba to be "murdered by bloodthirsty savages."[4] Enmegahbowh would continue the missionary efforts of St. Columba after Breck's departure in 1858 and was ordained deacon by Bishop Kemper in 1859 and in 1867 to the priesthood by Bishop Whipple.

It was after his abandonment of the St. Columba Mission that Breck turned to the establishment of what would become the cluster of educational institutions in Faribault. Breck initially called the institution he founded Bishop Seabury University. Here it bears repeating that there were not standard definitions for the terms used for higher education in the period prior to the Civil War. In using this term, Breck is envisioning the "university" not in its current understanding, as an institution that offers both undergraduate and graduate degrees, but as an umbrella organization that would include high school, college, preparation for ministry, and educational efforts among the Native American population. He chose Faribault as the location for the new incarnation of his missionary efforts because at the time it was one of the larger towns in Minnesota, and he noted that he hoped that it would one day be part of the railroad when it would eventually come through the region.[5] The first efforts of Breck's work was the creation of a primary

---

4. Quoted in Anderson, *Four Hundred Years*, 49.

5. Breck specifically notes in a letter that Faribault is on a "projected" railroad line (see Breck, *Life*, 364–65). The main railroads would eventually instead be built through St. Paul, with long-term consequences for the future development of the educational and diocesan complex in Faribault.

school, which from 1858 to 1859 was attended by fifteen local children, named the "Faribault Episcopal Institute of the Bishop Seabury University," while Breck began efforts at fundraising for the other efforts envisioned.[6]

Breck's early efforts would be transformed with the creation of the Diocese of Minnesota out of missionary bishop Jackson Kemper's vast missionary area and election of Henry Whipple as the first bishop of the diocese in 1859. Breck welcomed this development, seeing the bishop as chief missionary; he even lamented that one of the drawbacks to Nashotah was that it "ought to have had a bishop at its head."[7] In 1860, after Bishop Whipple's arrival, the entity in Faribault would be renamed and incorporated as the Bishop Seabury Mission. Breck's efforts at establishing a school in Faribault was essential in Whipple's decision to choose Faribault as his residence, and he specifically noted the ability for a future seminary to provide for clergy needs on the frontier: "it [choosing Faribault as his residence] offered me the prospect for the establishment of Church schools. Nashotah which I loved could not provide clergy needed for the growing West. After eighteen years we had but one Nashotah man among our clergy."[8]

With Bishop Whipple's choice of Faribault as his residence, another major development would be the decision to establish what would be the first cathedral in The Episcopal Church, in 1862. Whipple and Breck were in agreement that the cathedral would not be supported by endowments like English cathedrals, but instead would be home to a worshiping congregation and be the center of the missionary efforts envisioned in the state.

In the early 1860s, there were a functioning primary school and initial efforts to train a handful of clergy through directed reading.[9] As part of fundraising efforts, in the 1860s Breck pub-

---

6. See McElwain, Norwood, and Grant, "Seabury-Western Theological Seminary," 288.

7. Breck as quoted in Haugaard, "Missionary Vision of James Lloyd Breck," 245.

8. Whipple, *Light and Shadows*, 59–60.

9. It is a bit too much to claim, as Bishop McElwain does in his 1936 article,

lished a series of Missionary Papers. He would circulate these Missionary Papers through church networks, then periodically travel to cities on the East Coast as part of fundraising tours to support the efforts outlined in the pamphlets. In 1864, he laid out a vision for six different cohorts of students to be educated and trained in Faribault: "1) juveniles, 2) and 3) youth of both sexes, 4) young men up through the collegiate studies, 5) the Divinity Hall, and 6) the Indian school."[10] Breck's and Whipple's fundraising efforts would be successful, resulting in the building of the first Seabury Hall in 1864. As the 1860s progressed, we begin to see more concerted efforts at training persons for ministry: several faculty members were recruited, and a library with over forty-five hundred volumes was established. The first bachelor of divinity degree was awarded in 1866, and a warden for Seabury Hall had been appointed to give oversight and direction. A more formal secondary school for young men had been established. An Indian school, as envisioned by Breck, was also initially created, but was formally discontinued, for the chilling reason recounted by McElwain: "the mortality was so high that the whole project had to be dropped."[11]

We should keep in mind that both Breck and Whipple envisioned education for Native Americans as an essential component, along with conversion to Christianity, for "civilizing" the persons they repeatedly referred to as "savages." We can see in Breck's own recollections how these twin concepts of "civilization" and "Christianity" went hand in hand. Recounting his initial meetings with Enmegahbowh, Breck notes that when they first met Enmegahbowh had been living in a "wigwam" but later "built a house for himself, thus he began civilization along with his Christianity."[12]

---

that the two persons ordained deacon in 1860 while studying for a few months in Faribault were "the first graduating class of old Seabury" (McElwain, Norwood, and Grant, "Seabury-Western Theological Seminary," 291). We have no indication at all the two persons took any formal courses or received any kind of certificate, let alone a degree.

10. As quoted in Haugaard, "Missionary Vision of James Lloyd Breck," 247.

11. McElwain, Norwood, and Grant, "Seabury-Western Theological Seminary," 289.

12. Breck, *Life*, 483.

While Bishop Whipple would intervene on several occasions to protest treatment of Native Americans, he was an enthusiastic participant in the cultural genocide of Native peoples through the emphasis on using education as a means to "civilizing." These were part of broader efforts at placing an emphasis on assimilation of Native Americans to settled, European understandings of "civilization." These efforts deliberately and consciously focused on youth: adults were considered set in their ways, so there were concerted efforts to remove Native American children from their families and place them in residential schools. This was an intentional cultural genocide, as the children were not permitted to use their tribal names, were disciplined if they spoke their tribal languages, and were required to adopt Christianity.[13] As the Faribault experiment also shows, these residential schools often resulted in literal genocide: diseases such as tuberculosis, scarlet fever, and measles often ran rampant in crowded and unsanitary conditions. Families at times had their children forcibly taken from them at the beginning of a semester, never to return.

By 1867, the vision was beginning to come into place: the schools planned by Breck had been established, the first bachelor of divinity was awarded, the cathedral that was seen as the center to mission work was being built, and the first dedicated seminary building had been erected. Yet it is precisely at this time that Breck resigned all of his positions to leave for California. Breck's departure is likely due to two factors. One was his missionary restlessness for seeking an ever new frontier, a trait he shared with Bishop Chase. The second was tension with Bishop Whipple concerning oversight and eventual direction of the mission efforts. Despite Breck's tireless efforts in organizing the schools, outlining a vision in his series of Missionary Papers, giving over 135 lectures to groups on the East Coast to raise funds, Whipple barely mentions him in his own autobiography with regard to the establishment of the Seabury Mission, lumping him in with a list of others involved:

---

13. See Anderson, *Education for Extinction*, for an historical overview, including the role of Christian missionary efforts.

The Bishop Seabury Mission was organized in 1860. Some of my dearest friends doubted our success in the undertaking and declined to become trustees. The Rev. E. R. Welles, the Rev. D. B. Knickerbacker, the Rev. E. G. Gear, the Rev. S. Y. McMasters, the Rev. James Dobbin, the Rev. S. W. Manney, the Rev. T. B. Welles, the Rev. J. L. Breck, the Rev. J. S. Kedney of the clergy, and H. T. Welles, E. T. Wilder, Isaac Atwater, and Harvey Officer of the laity, and the trustees elected at a later period never failed to hold up my hands. They believed that it was God's work, and they knew how to labor and to wait.[14]

And despite Breck laying out a vision for schools for young women as well as young men to be part of a future complex of educational institutions in Faribault, Whipple credits himself: "In 1866, feeling the necessity of a school for the education of the daughters of the clergy, notwithstanding the burdens which we were carrying, I determined to begin a school in my own home."[15] Haugaard notes that in Whipple's autobiography "Breck appears, but fleetingly; politely recalled, with little warmth."[16] There is no real "smoking gun" in the extant writings of either Breck or Whipple to give any deeper or further insight into their relationship. There does appear to have been some tension with Breck's role as "dean" in the structure of the Bishop Seabury Mission, the umbrella corporation under which the various schools were organized (starting in 1864 the Divinity School had an appointed warden to provide oversight of that institution). McElwain notes that minutes from the board of trustees ask Dr. Breck to "cooperate" with the warden of Seabury and the rector of Shattuck School, and that a committee was established to define the rights and roles of the rector of Shattuck.[17] While primary and secondary sources do not provide in-depth details, we do know that Breck departed for California and rarely mentioned Whipple or his former

14. Whipple, *Light and Shadows*, 188–89.
15. Whipple, *Light and Shadows*, 189.
16. Haugaard, "Missionary Vision of James Lloyd Breck," 249.
17. McElwain, Norwood, and Grant, "Seabury-Western Theological Seminary," 294.

missionary efforts in Minnesota; and that Whipple's characterizations in his own later autobiography do not reflect the depth of Breck's involvement in the establishment of the Bishop Seabury Mission and the suite of educational institutions that would be formed, including Bishop Seabury Divinity School.

Growth of Bishop Seabury Divinity School

The academic year 1866–1867 marked a significant turning point in the life of the Bishop Seabury Mission. Breck departed for California, and the first degrees of bachelor of divinity were awarded. The educational institutions Breck envisioned took shape: Shattuck Hall was constructed as the school for young men, and St. Mary's Hall was established as the school for young women. Bishop Seabury Divinity School, as it now begins regularly to be referred to in the sources, continued to grow. The seminary was buffeted by many of the usual challenges facing institutions of higher education in the second half of the 1800s: for instance, the original Seabury Hall burned to the ground and a replacement had to be constructed. It was dedicated on Thanksgiving Day in 1873, establishing an annual tradition of a Thanksgiving dinner and prayer service for the school. In 1870, William Jason Gold was brought to the seminary as professor of exegesis and would provide a crucial link between Seabury and Western Seminary. Gold left Seabury Divinity School in 1873 to teach classics at Racine College, before being called in 1885 to Western Seminary in Chicago, where he taught liturgy until his death in 1903.

Students seeking to study for the ministry but who did not have the necessary background from undergraduate studies (which at this time involved Greek, Latin, Hebrew, and introductory biblical studies) were able to study in the Preparatory Department at Shattuck School. It was not uncommon for secondary schools at this time to offer some courses considered to be a college level, as either preparation for vocational training or for graduates to transfer to another institution to complete a bachelor's degree. There was a similar parallel with Nashotah House, with students preparing for ministry but lacking elements of schooling often sent to nearby St. John's Military Academy and later to Racine College.[18] Moving into the twentieth century, with the advent of accreditation and the increasing distinctions made between high school, undergraduate, and graduate education, Bishop Seabury ended the Preparatory Department at Shattuck and inaugurated a collaborative program with nearby Carleton College. Though established by the Congregational Church, there had always been a substantive Episcopal presence at Carleton, and the creation of a collaborative partnership was further fostered by ecumenical discussions between the Congregational Church and The Episcopal Church in the 1920s.[19] Under the arrangement, students would need to meet Carleton's standards and attend Carleton for two years in residence for the necessary background coursework, at which point they would move to Seabury, allowing for the completion of an undergraduate bachelor's degree and the bachelor of divinity in six years rather than seven.

The program lasted for over a decade, and there was an increasingly close relationship between the dioceses in Minnesota,[20] Bishop Seabury, and Carleton. An Episcopal chaplain was appointed at Carleton who was also rector of the local Episcopal church, and nearly twenty Carleton faculty members (including three who were ordained) were Episcopalian. The relationship was so close that Bishop McElwain, former warden at Seabury and later elected bishop of Minnesota, wanted to relocate Bishop Seabury Divinity School to Northfield in the early 1930s. The onset of the Great Depression, and ensuing financial difficulties, made it too difficult to consider new buildings for Bishop Seabury in Northfield, resulting

---

18. See mention in McElwain, Norwood, and Grant, "Seabury-Western Theological Seminary," 301, and the more in-depth discussion in Gundersen, "Experiment in 'Christian Co-operation,'" 444–54.

19. Gundersen, "Experiment in 'Christian Co-operation,'" 446.

20. The Missionary District of Duluth was created out of the Diocese of Minnesota in 1895, and was admitted to General Convention in 1907, eventually subsumed again into the Diocese of Minnesota in 1944. It was also a signatory to the arrangement with Carleton.

in Bishop McElwain instead turning to Western Seminary in 1931 to begin discussions around a potential merger.

Part of the impetus in seeking to relocate the school to Northfield, and eventually to merge with Western Seminary, had to do with changes in both Minnesota and higher education. With regard to changes in Minnesota, while Faribault had been chosen because of its size and location to be the home of both the cathedral and the Bishop Seabury University, the town would soon be left behind as Minnesota grew and developed. The hoped-for railroad line that Breck mentioned was routed through Minneapolis-St. Paul instead. Along with being located on the Mississippi River, this resulted in phenomenal growth for the twin cities, leaving Faribault behind. In 1860, Faribault had roughly 3,000 residents; St. Paul, 20,000; and Minneapolis, 13,000. Thirty years later, in 1890, Minneapolis had 164,000 residents; St. Paul, 133,000; and Faribault had 6,500.[21] Breck's hopes that Faribault would become an important center in Minnesota did not come to fruition.

Changes in higher education and theological education were also impacting Seabury Divinity School. The late 1800s and early 1900s saw increasing trends toward professionalization in the ministry, with emphasis on an undergraduate bachelor's degree as a foundation for preparation for seminary training. The model in Faribault, with ministry students taking courses at what was essentially a high school, was increasingly a thing of the past. The collaborative program with Carleton was an effort to address this concern, and the opportunity for relocating Seabury to Northfield would have been a potential solution. But the Great Depression made the ask for raising money and building the campus needed for Seabury in Northfield too daunting. Western Seminary, which was located in a thriving urban area, had developed a similar collaborative partnership with Northwestern,[22] and which already had a campus in 1933, addressed the main concerns facing Seabury Divinity School.

---

21. Wikipedia, "Faribault, Minnesota"; "Saint Paul, Minnesota."
22. Gundersen, "Experiment in 'Christian Co-operation,'" 448.

BEGINNINGS

In its roughly seventy years of existence, Bishop Seabury Divinity School educated about four hundred persons for ordained ministry, the majority serving in the Midwest, including two bishops of Minnesota and a bishop of the Diocese of Kansas.[23] As The Episcopal Church was increasingly marked by divisions between high church/Anglo-Catholic and low church parties, Bishop Whipple, at least, set the intention not to commit the seminary to any particular party: "it has been my wish to train up men whose faith should be firm as the eternal truths of the Catholic Creed, and whose love and charity should be as broad as the Church is broad. I do not want, and God helping me, will not have here a training school for any party."[24] Despite this quotation from Whipple, Seabury Divinity did trend toward the low church spectrum of the church; a longtime Seabury-Western faculty member noted that when he arrived in the 1960s older faculty had told him it took nearly twenty years after the merger of 1933 for the "chapel wars" to subside and reconcile the more low church liturgical style of Seabury Divinity with the more high church traditions of Western Seminary.[25]

As noted when beginning the survey of Seabury Divinity School, its founding was inextricably linked with James Lloyd Breck's missionary work among Native Americans in Minnesota, and there had been an initial plan for an "Indian School" among Breck's vision for the collection of educational institutions to be founded in Faribault. These plans did not materialize, in part due to what the Anglo resources refer to as the "mortality" involved, as well as the "constraints" of civilization. Yet there continued to be a residual aspect of this outreach to Native American communities in Seabury's DNA. Sherman Coolidge, the first Arapahoe priest, attended Seabury, was the first Native American clergyperson to receive the bachelor of divinity degree from an Episcopal seminary, and was ordained by Bishop Whipple in 1884.[26] The first American

23. "Seventy Years," 15.
24. As quoted in "Seventy Years," 20.
25. Interview with Newland Smith, April 16, 2024.
26. See Anderson, *400 Years*, 229. Degree confirmation through Bishop

Indian bishop, Harold Jones, attended Seabury-Western just after the creation of the school in 1933 and was ordained deacon in 1938.[27] But apart from these few, it would not be until the 1980s that Seabury-Western would make a concerted effort to engage in theological education with Native Americans.

Western Seminary, 1883–1933

The establishment of a training school for clergy in Chicago in 1883 was the result of a longstanding desire by Bishop William McLaren of the Diocese of Chicago, and over the course of his lengthy episcopate (1875–1905) he would profoundly shape what would become Western Seminary. The need for a seminary reflects the astonishing growth in the Midwest due to industrialization, urbanization, and the spread of railroads. Chicago grew from 30,000 in 1850 to 112,000 in 1860, 300,000 in 1870, 500,000 in 1880, and over one million by 1900.[28] Bishop McLaren renewed a call for the establishment of a seminary to meet the needs of a growing church in his address to the Diocesan Convention of 1883. The establishment of the seminary was made possible due to the patronage of Tolman Wheeler, who donated land near the intersection of Washington Boulevard and California Avenue, in what is now the East Garfield Park neighborhood, as well as one hundred thousand dollars for the construction of buildings and one hundred thousand dollars toward an endowment. The two hundred thousand dollar gift is equivalent to nearly six million dollars, adjusted for inflation.

Wheeler's gifts made possible the creation of a training school for ministry, which was in its formation a collaborative effort between the recently created dioceses in Illinois.[29] It was

---

Seabury Divinity School Student Register, Bexley Seabury Seminary Federation Archives.

27. Anderson, *400 Years*, 118.

28. Wikipedia, "Demographics of Chicago."

29. In 1877, the Diocese of Illinois, comprising the entire state, was divided into the Dioceses of Chicago, Springfield, and Quincy.

intended to be a regional seminary, with the bishops of Chicago, Quincy, Springfield, Fond du Lac, and Indiana listed among the incorporators and given seats as trustees. Unlike Whipple's stated vision for Seabury Divinity School not to be "a training school for any party," the founding vision for Western Seminary was quite different. Its stated purpose was for "the education of fit persons in the Catholic faith in its purity and integrity, as taught in the Holy Scriptures, held by the Primitive Church, summed up in the Creeds, and affirmed by the undisputed General Councils,"[30] planting it firmly within the Anglo-Catholic and high church wing of The Episcopal Church. Yet the founders of Western Seminary also saw it as the regional seminary for the Midwest, which included a number of Anglo-Catholic dioceses. The diocesan Committee on Western Seminary reported to the 1886 Diocesan Convention of Chicago that "experience has demonstrated the advantages which institutions of this character enjoy when located near such centers of influence and population [i.e., growing urban areas] and that in the very nature of things, the Western Theological Seminary must become to the West and Northwest what the General Seminary is to the East."[31] Yet despite this appeal, over the course of its existence, Western Theological Seminary would draw nearly three-quarters of its students from the dioceses in the state of Illinois, the Diocese of Indiana, and the Diocese of Fond du Lac.

The seminary opened for instruction in the fall of 1885 with nine students, and for nearly the next twenty years Bishop McLaren would exercise enormous oversight over the operations and development of Western Seminary—an oversight which led to the seminary becoming practically defunct in the final years of his episcopacy. Instructors were recruited, including Francis Hall, who would later become dean at General Seminary, and student enrollment remained steady. Yet Bishop McLaren's refusal to cede

30. As quoted in McElwain, Norwood, and Grant, "Seabury-Western Theological Seminary," 302.

31. "An Appeal to the Friends of Theological Education in the West, for the West," Committee on Western Theological Seminary to the 1886 Diocesan Convention of the Diocese of Chicago, Bexley Seabury Seminary Federation Archives.

any oversight or authority profoundly hampered the school. He appointed a warden but retained the title of dean. In his history of the seminary, Norwood notes that "in the academic sense there was no faculty," since they did not meet regularly or coordinate curriculum. Rather, as Hall later recalled, the instructors were more akin to "tutors in a private school" presided over by the bishop.[32] By 1901, McLaren was ailing and had been bishop for over twenty-five years. He still retained oversight over the school but was too infirm to engage in fundraising. He retained his post as dean but was unable to provide any real day-to-day governance. The seminary was barely functioning, largely due to financial shortfalls. Several instructors were dismissed, and others left to join other institutions. Francis Hall continued as the sole instructor with a handful of students. During the 1904–1905 academic year, the seminary ceased to operate.

It was during this initial phase that Western Seminary would enroll its first students of color, through connections with the Nippon Sei Ko Kai (the Holy Catholic Church of Japan). The Nippon Sei Ko Kai was formed in 1887 through the merger of missionary jurisdictions of The Episcopal Church and the Church of England, creating the first province of the Anglican Communion that was not of European or Caucasian descent.[33] The Rev. John Kichinosuke Ochiai is listed as a graduate in the class of 1898, with at least two other clergy from the Nippon Sei Ko Kai graduating prior to 1923 and the seminary's relocation to Evanston.

In 1905, Bishop Anderson succeeded Bishop McLaren and revitalized Western Seminary over the next several years. New faculty were recruited, a dean was appointed and ceded authority over the day-to-day affairs of the school, and significant bequests were courted and received. One of these bequests was from Charles Hale, bishop of Springfield, who provided the equivalent

---

32. As recounted in McElwain, Norwood, and Grant, "Seabury-Western Theological Seminary," 303.

33. By the early 1900s, a majority of the clergy were of Japanese descent and not foreign missionaries, but it would not be until 1923 that the first persons of Japanese descent would be elected bishop.

of over one million dollars to endow a lecture series. Provisions of the bequest also required the lectures to be printed, bound, and sent to seminaries and bishops across the church. The Hale Lectures would become an enormous contribution to scholarship in the Anglican world. In a more idiosyncratic turn of events, a prominent Chicago benefactor, Lydia Gold Hibbard, would provide a bequest for the establishment of an Egyptian and Near Eastern studies library whose collection, for a time, would rival other museums in Chicago. A promotional pamphlet published by Western around 1915 solemnly noted that the collection included fragments from the tomb of Ramses II, thus "bearing witness to the historicity of a contested portion of the book of Exodus."[34]

Given the vigorous fundraising by the dean, William DeWitt, and Bishop Anderson, several new buildings were constructed, including a dean's residence. The same promotional pamphlet describing Ramses II's tomb also proudly notes the installation of running water into the dormitory originally constructed in 1885, adroitly noting that "a toilet room of sufficient capacity is in each dormitory, and is usually preferred to a portable bowl and pitcher."[35] Eventually the seminary would introduce what was repeatedly referred to in sources of the time as a "West Point Plan," whereby students would attend free of charge.[36]

Formation of Seabury-Western Theological Seminary, 1933

Yet this period of growth would soon run up against something over which the seminary would have no control: the continued impact of the rapid development of Chicago as an industrialized and urban center. Norwood notes in his history that the location of Western Seminary, near the intersection of Washington and California, in what is now known as the East Garfield Park

34. *Illustrated Historical Sketch*, 28.
35. *Illustrated Historical Sketch*, 8.
36. *Illustrated Historical Sketch*, 36; McElwain, Norwood, and Grant, "Seabury-Western Theological Seminary," 305, also uses the term "West Point Plan."

neighborhood, had been "on the outskirts of the city" in 1885 and was, by the 1910s, "becoming increasingly undesirable." On the one hand, this reflects the impact of the extension of the electrified elevated train to the neighborhood and the increase in commercialization. In addition to the extension of public transportation, the Sears corporation opened a massive factory and distribution center. Yet this also reflects changing demographics: no doubt concerns about the neighborhood becoming "undesirable" were a result of what had been primarily a white neighborhood first receiving an influx of Eastern European Russian Jews and Italian immigrants, and, during the First World War, significant African American immigration. The burst of new building in the 1900s, renovations to the original 1885 structures, and expansion of the faculty also seems to have caught up with Western. The promotional pamphlet published in the 1910s concludes with a fundraising pitch, stating that the seminary was "under the great disadvantage of inadequate endowments" and that "The Western faces a deficit annually of considerable amount."[37] The seminary would then suffer another setback, when the rental income from a downtown property dedicated to its support would be unavailable due to the major rebuilding that Wacker Avenue inaugurated in the 1920s.

In 1923, the board of trustees decided to suspend operations of the seminary and pursue relocation to Evanston, due to offers of land from Northwestern University and Garrett Biblical on which to build. The seminary would then run into a roadblock due to an ordinance adopted by the city of Evanston to prohibit dormitory building in the area donated to Western Seminary. The board twice appealed the matter all the way to the Illinois Supreme Court, but the legal process took five years, so that it was not until 1927 that Western Seminary resumed operations. The previous five years had been spent on fundraising and on the legal appeals process. After winning both appeals to the Illinois Supreme Court, construction of the new buildings began in 1928, with the seminary temporarily operating out of St. Mark's Episcopal Church in

---

37. *Illustrated Historical Sketch*, 36. This source also routinely refers to the seminary as "The Western."

Evanston in the interim. As the seminary buildings were gradually completed, Western shifted to its location to Sheridan Road, sharing classroom and chapel space with Garrett. By 1932, there were eight faculty members and fifty students enrolled, and the first dedicated buildings opened.

No sooner had Western Seminary reopened in its new location when discussions of merger with Bishop Seabury Divinity School began. As noted above, Bishop Seabury Divinity School was facing a significant financial shortfall, combined with the fact that its main buildings had been constructed in the 1870s and by the 1930s were in need of renovation. An initial estimate of a five hundred thousand dollar capital campaign was increased to a one million dollar capital campaign. Conversations concerning merger were initiated by the Rev. Addison Knickerbocker, a Western alumnus who was serving as a priest in the Diocese of Minnesota, in conversations with Frederick Grant, the dean of Western Seminary.[38] Grant conferred with the Western Seminary board, and Knickerbocker reported back to Bishop Keeler (coadjutor of Minnesota) and Bishop McElwain (diocesan), who in turn initiated a discussion with the board of trustees of the Bishop Seabury Mission. Both seminaries appointed representatives to a joint committee, which began discussions in May of 1932. As one contemporary to the conversations assessed the situation: "Western had buildings and Seabury had endowment income" to support student scholarships.[39]

Yet there would be some internal divisions of the precise nature of that endowment income. As the merger conversations continued, the Bishop Seabury board of trustees received two conflicting reports from two different attorneys: one attorney consulted by the board claimed the restriction on the endowments would not permit it to be used in support of a joint seminary, while on the other hand the chancellor of Diocese of Minnesota stated that it was possible. The confusion arose from the nature of the corporation itself: the Bishop Seabury Mission was the

---

38. Johnson, "History," 1–2.
39. Johnson, "History," 4.

umbrella organization that included not only Bishop Seabury Divinity School but also Shattuck Hall, St. Mary's School, and other endeavors in the diocese. To address these conflicting opinions, a compromise was made so that the funds restricted for theological education would not be transferred to the new school but would still be controlled by the Bishop Seabury Mission—but also that the bylaws of the new institution would specifically direct that these funds would be in support of the new institution.[40]

With the question of the endowments resolved, additional concerns were raised by the Bishop Seabury Divinity community. One concern had to do with the small parishes and missions in proximity to Faribault that had been served by faculty at the seminary.[41] Another had to do with the issue of church parties; Western Seminary was still closely associated with the historically high church Diocese of Chicago, while Bishop Keeler was part of the low church party in The Episcopal Church.[42] An important factor in the merger was the support of both Bishop McElwain and Bishop Keeler. Bishop McElwain was the former warden at Bishop Seabury, and current diocesan bishop in Minnesota, while Keeler had been elected coadjutor for the Diocese of Minnesota in 1931. In his address to the diocesan Convention in 1934 Keeler noted: "When the merger was first proposed, I am frank to say I was opposed to it. But a careful study of Seabury's financial status and a thorough understanding of the conditions under which the merger is to be effected led me very definitely to see the advantages in the project."[43] Yet the vote was not unanimous: the final vote of the Seabury trustees was eight in favor, four opposed. The reason for the opposition was that some of the Seabury trustees wanted a time-certain or time-defined component to the creation

---

40. Letter from Bishop Stephen Keeler to Dean Frederick Grant, May 20, 1932, Bexley Seabury Seminary Federation Archives.

41. Johnson, "History," 4.

42. A profile of Bishop Keeler specifically states that although he went to General Seminary he was "not an Anglo-Catholic"; see Noble, "Portrait of Bishop Keeler," 13–14.

43. Johnson, "History," 6.

of the new seminary, to be reassessed after an initial period, while the majority of the Seabury trustees and the Western trustees did not agree with this amendment to the proposed bylaws of the new seminary. As McElwain noted,

> Several gentlemen voted in the negative, not because they did not agree with the principle of the union of the schools (which they did), but because they disliked to have the corporation [i.e., the Bishop Seabury Mission, the umbrella corporation of Bishop Seabury Divinity School] tied up to a contract which . . . is 'in perpetuity.' We explained to them that any further amendment would necessitate delay and possible rejection . . . . I am sorry that there is this little rift in our board, but do not regard it as serious, for to all but one of the objectors I know that the general idea was very acceptable to them.[44]

In the fall of 1933, after little more than a year of conversations, the newly merged and named Seabury-Western Theological Seminary welcomed its first class of students.

---

44. McElwain, letter to Grant, April 19, 1933, Bexley Seabury Seminary Federation Archives. The 8–4 vote is recorded in a telegram sent by McElwain to Grant on April 18, 1933; Bexley Seabury Seminary Federation Archives.

CHAPTER 3

Bexley Hall Seminary, 1968–2012

BEXLEY HALL BEGAN ITS new incarnation as a constituent member of Colgate Rochester Divinity School in the fall of 1968.[1] Given that Bexley Hall had seen its share of difficulties over the course of its history, it is important to note that the relocation to Rochester was not a result of the seminary's struggles. Enrollment was robust, and the faculty was fully staffed. Relocation was a result of on the one hand changes that Kenyon College felt it needed to make, and on the other hand an effort by Bexley better to serve the church by relocating to an urban and ecumenical context. Bexley faculty member Richard Spielmann, who lived through the relocation and served on the various committees that brought it about, summarized it best when he wrote, "The right thing [e.g., relocating to an

---

1. Overall, this chapter is slightly shorter than the other chapters in this history. This is not due to the lack of significant aspects of Bexley Hall's history in Rochester but is in turn a reflection of the available source materials. Bexley Hall did not publish its own catalog or have its own faculty or board of trustees. The board of CRCDS served as the board of Bexley Hall, and the CRCDS president was the president of Bexley Hall. There are, in turn, significant gaps in the written records that Bexley Hall kept, in part due to its several relocations and restructurings during this period. There simply is not the availability of primary sources for this period as there is with Seabury-Western, or even with Bexley Hall prior to its move to Rochester in 1968. This chapter relies significantly on interviews from students and faculty from the 1968–2012 period.

urban and ecumenical setting] was done for the wrong reasons [because Kenyon no longer wanted a seminary]."[2]

Bexley's move to Rochester was part of a broader effort to create the Rochester Center for Theological Studies, which was incorporated in 1968 and intended to be an umbrella organization for the hoped-for future ecumenical partnership to be created by CRDS, Bexley Hall, and St. Bernard's, the local Roman Catholic seminary. There were other movements in this direction during the 1960s. The Graduate Theological Union had been formed in 1962, a consortium of seminaries in Berkeley, California, that maintained their independence yet collaborated on joint master's and doctoral programs. Yet the Rochester Center would never fully come to fruition; while St. Bernard's would be located for a time on the CRCDS campus and become an affiliated member, and there would be cross-registration for courses, the kind of holistic integration into an ecumenical center would never be realized. We can see a glimpse of the vision for this ecumenical center in a letter from Bishop Nelson Burroughs of the Diocese of Ohio sent to donors announcing Bexley's move. Bishop Burroughs noted,

> In Rochester, Bexley will retain its full identity as an Episcopal seminary, yet be integrated to the greatest possible extent with Colgate Rochester, an interdenominational seminary, with St. Bernard's, a Roman Catholic one, and doubtless others who will come together in the next few years to form what may be known as the Rochester Center for Theological Studies. I have every reason to believe that the bishops, clergy, and people of the Episcopal Church will rejoice in this pace-setting venture.[3]

Alas, along with St. Bernard's never fully integrating itself into the consortium, only one additional school would eventually join. Itself the result of the merger of the Baptist seminaries formerly affiliated with the University of Rochester and Colgate University, CRDS would be joined in 1970 by another Baptist seminary, the

---

2. Spielmann, *Bexley Hall, 150 Years*, 96.
3. December 7, 1967, letter from Bishop Nelson Burroughs to donors to the Lichtenberg Library Fund, Bexley Seabury Seminary Federation Archives.

freestanding Crozer Baptist Theological Seminary, to create Colgate Rochester Crozer Divinity School.[4]

The vision for Bexley Hall's relationship with CRDS is laid out in the 1968 agreement establishing the merger. The agreement lists a number of "considerations" that inform the partnership. The agreement specifically cites the importance of its "urban environment," noting that "since ninety per cent of the American people will live in or near metropolitan centers in the foreseeable future, the place to prepare persons for ministry is the environment in which they will carry on their ministry." The ecumenical setting is also lifted up: "There is a growing conviction that the best theological education takes place within an ecumenical setting. The plan for joint operations provides a structure for continuous and creative encounter between the Anglican and Puritan-Protestant traditions in a way that will enrich and strengthen both. The plan also envisages an affiliation with St. Bernard's Seminary of the Roman Catholic Church in a Rochester Center for Theological Studies." The agreement also cites financial reasons, noting that cooperation and collaboration will help offset the fact that "the cost of theological education has roughly doubled every ten years during the past three decades."[5]

Bexley Hall would, in essence, be subsumed into CRCDS and function as a kind of Department of Episcopal and Anglican Studies. Bexley Hall was incorporated as an educational not for profit in New York State with its own board of trustees for that corporation, but that board had no control over the faculty or curriculum. The emphasis, overall, was on the creation of a single, unified entity. Bexley Hall funds were pooled and incorporated into the single budget of CRDS, with the exception of funds with specific restrictions, which could be appropriated and used by Bexley Hall.

---

4. Prior to 1970, I will use CRDS (Colgate Rochester Divinity School); after 1970, when Crozer relocated and joined the cluster, I will use CRCDS (Colgate Rochester Crozer Divinity School). It is common to still see CRDS used in seminary publications in the 1970s and even into the 1980s; CRCDS does not seem to be consistently used by the seminary itself until the 1980s.

5. "Agreement Between Bexley Hall and Colgate Rochester Divinity School," July 17, 1968. Bexley Seabury Seminary Federation Archives.

The president of CRDS would be the president of Bexley Hall and head of the Joint Faculty, and the treasurer of CRDS would be the treasurer for Bexley Hall. There was a single faculty and a single curriculum, and all Bexley Hall faculty were considered CRDS faculty. Degrees could be awarded based on a student's choice. An Episcopal student could choose to receive a CRDS degree or a Bexley Hall degree. All library materials and resources Bexley brought to the partnership would be held within the CRDS library. The 1968 agreement also stated there would be no distinctions made between students, with uniform standards of admission and an emphasis on common worship, and that students would be housed without regard to denominational affiliation.

The agreement also set parameters for preserving a distinctive identity for Bexley Hall within CRDS. The board of trustees created for Bexley Hall essentially had three functions. It appointed the dean of Bexley Hall (normally chosen from one of the existing faculty), it could award Bexley Hall degrees to those students who chose to receive a Bexley MDiv instead of a CRCDS MDiv, and it could direct the use of specifically restricted endowments. In 1974, the Association of Theological Schools maintained Bexley's own accreditation by virtue of its partnership with CRCDS, similar to the relationship between Berkeley Divinity School and Yale Divinity School. This accreditation was renewed in 1983 and 1993. The agreement also granted that Bexley Hall would have "full membership" in the hoped-for Rochester Center for Theological Studies, and would have its own, separate alumni association.

The 1968 agreement was clear that Bexley Hall would be fully incorporated into CRDS, and that there would be a single institution with a single faculty, curriculum, and student body while, at the same time, preserving a distinct identity for Bexley Hall. As a former dean put it, "I was more or less the Chair of the Department of Anglican and Episcopal Studies at Colgate Rochester."[6]

Bexley Hall soon encountered "some familiar problems":[7] namely, financial and enrollment struggles. Bexley had seen fairly

---

6. Interview with William Petersen, March 11, 2024.
7. Spielmann, *Bexley Hall, 150 Years*, 106.

robust enrollment in the 1960s. This was something shared widely across theological education, a combination of post–World War II expansion in Mainline Protestant denominations and a boost in enrollment due to the Vietnam War and the availability of student deferments from the selective service. The minutes from the very first meeting of the new board of trustees for Bexley Hall noted that there was a need to communicate more clearly with bishops that Bexley had not closed and to advocate for the advantages of preparing for ministry in an urban, ecumenical theological center. There continued to be significant financial deficits, and in the fall of 1973 only three students enrolled in the master of divinity program.

Bexley also began to address issues of diversity, equity, and inclusion in its new setting. After William Alston graduated in 1859, only a handful of African American students attended Bexley prior to 1968. Kenyon did not admit its first African Americans until 1952 and did not admit women students until 1969. In Bexley's very first academic year in Rochester, African American students occupied the main administration building, Strong Hall, for three weeks in March of 1969. At the time, there were five students of color at Bexley Hall (four African American, one Hispanic/Latinx) who were members of the CRDS Black Caucus. In the 1968–1969 academic year, there was only one African American trustee (out of thirty-six persons on the CRDS board of trustees) and only one African American faculty member. After several weeks of discussion and negotiation, CRCDS agreed to have African Americans make up one-third of its trustees, to hire more faculty of color, and to establish a Black Church studies program. The Black Church studies program included the recruitment of African American faculty, offering courses specifically geared toward the African American experience, and provided internships in both churches and social service agencies working in African American communities. The establishment of the Black Church studies program became a draw for African American students, both in the Baptist traditions that formed CRCDS and for Bexley Hall. The result was that throughout the 1970s and 1980s, despite routinely being one of the smaller Episcopal seminaries, Bexley Hall would regularly have among the highest number of African American students enrolled (by percentage of total enrollment).

Bexley Hall had enrolled fewer than six female students total prior to 1968, all of them as special students not enrolled in degree programs, and did not have any women graduates at all in its 144 years in Gambier. This was due largely to the fact that prior to 1968, Bexley Hall required that one had to be a postulant for holy orders and sponsored by a diocese in order to attend. Since The Episcopal Church would not formally approve women to be ordained as deacons until 1970, there were no female postulants. This would change after 1970, and a number of women students enrolled at Bexley Hall in Rochester, with the seminary overwhelmingly supportive of women's ordination. Bishop Robert Spears, elected bishop of Rochester in 1970, was supportive of women's ordination. Bishop George Barrett, bishop at the time of Bexley's affiliation with CRDS (who retired in 1969) was supportive of women's ordination, and in 1975 would preside at the ordinations of four women to the priesthood in Washington, DC, a year before the 1976 General Convention approved the ordination of women. By 1975, over fourteen women students had enrolled. The first dean in Rochester, retired bishop William Corrigan, was a supporter of women's ordination and was one of the three bishops who presided at the ordinations of the Philadelphia Eleven in 1974. Two of the eleven women deacons ordained in 1974 were graduates of Bexley Hall: Merrill Bittner and Betty Bone Scheiss. One of the women ordained with the Washington Four in September of 1975, Betty Rosenberg Powell, was the first woman to receive a doctor of ministry degree in The Episcopal Church, graduating from Bexley Hall in 1975. Soon after the relocation to Rochester, Carol Doran would become the first female faculty member at CRCDS from the Episcopal/Anglican tradition.[8]

8. Given that there was a single faculty and single student body, it's difficult to state that Bexley Hall admitted its first women students or hired its first female faculty member—faculty were CRCDS faculty, hired by CRCDS, and students were admitted to CRCDS through the CRCDS admissions process. Yet students could choose to affiliate with Bexley and receive a Bexley degree,

Through the 1970s and 1980s, Bexley Hall would develop several distinctive elements to its program of formation as part of CRCDS. As it had been in Ohio, Bexley would continue to be generally a regional seminary, with the majority of its students coming from Central New York, Rochester, Western New York, and parts of Ohio and Pennsylvania, and would continue to have a strong relationship with the local diocese, with the bishop of Rochester serving on Bexley's board of trustees.

It would develop a strong sense of identity as a program of formation within an ecumenical community, an element that would continue to develop with the eventual formation of a partnership with Trinity Lutheran Seminary in the late 1990s. Bexley students and faculty from this period consistently noted the importance of this ecumenical formation as an Anglican/Episcopal community within the broader CRCDS landscape. With a single faculty, curriculum, and student body, students and faculty studied, worshiped, and lived together. Students spoke particularly of the importance of developing a sense of Episcopal identity as a minority in a larger Baptist seminary, saying it gave them a stronger and clearer understanding of who they were as Episcopalians. The role of worship and liturgy was particularly important in helping shape and preserve an Episcopal identity and Episcopal community within CRCDS. Bexley introduced the Triduum services for Holy Week and Easter to the CRCDS chapel and held its own weekly community eucharistic service and prayed the Daily Offices, alongside the regular schedule of worship for CRCDS. While other elements of the hoped-for ecumenical Rochester Center for Theological Studies never did come to fruition, this emphasis on ecumenical formation became a central aspect of Bexley Hall as part of CRCDS.

Bexley would also begin to develop adaptive programs for theological education and formation. In the 1980s, Bexley would shift to become predominantly a commuter school. While continuing to have full-time, residential students, the majority would be

---

and faculty could choose to be considered as part of the Episcopal/Anglican faculty within CRCDS.

non-residential, largely second career persons, who would commute to campus. Class scheduling was reorganized to reflect this, clustering courses on certain days of the week to accommodate students with full-time jobs. This would eventually become widespread and more widely adopted across theological education, but Bexley would be a pioneer in this kind of curricular reorganization. Bexley Hall would also continue to provide opportunities for women in ministry. Throughout the 1980s, the Diocese of Albany was one of the dioceses of The Episcopal Church that did not ordain women to the priesthood and did not permit ordained women to serve as priests in the diocese. Women from Albany seeking ordination could be sponsored through the Diocese of Rochester and attend Bexley Hall at CRCDS.[9]

Beginning in the late 1980s, and into the 1990s, Bexley Hall would also begin to develop low-residency training programs with diocesan partners. Having courses meeting over weekends, or in short-term, week-long intensives, is now commonplace among Episcopal seminaries but was extremely rare in an era when most students were either residential or commuters and courses were held onsite. In the late 1980s, Bexley received a grant from the Lilly Endowment and developed a program for theological education with the Diocese of West Virginia. Faculty would travel to West Virginia and offer courses over weekends for persons preparing for ministry. These efforts would also draw in students from other nearby dioceses, including Ohio, Southern Ohio, and Lexington. As one faculty member put it, "It was one of the first times that we went to them, and did not expect students to come to us, and provided for-credit, degree granting courses in low residency models."[10] These efforts helped to strengthen relationships and partnerships with neighboring dioceses, while at the same time allowing for preparation for ministry for students who otherwise would be unable to attend, due to work and family commitments.

Bexley Hall in the 1970s, 1980s, and 1990s was marked by a profound commitment to formation and training for ministry

---

9. Interview with Ellen Wondra, March 13, 2024.
10. Interview with Ellen Wondra, March 13, 2024.

within an ecumenical context, and to developing innovative, collaborative pathways for training for ministry. Both of these aspects would be important components of Bexley's identity as it entered into a period of profound transition and change in the period from 1998–2012.

Yet the Rochester years would also reflect longstanding unresolved issues and tensions. Conversations with students and faculty from the Rochester years consistently name the same ongoing tensions in four areas: budget, faculty, library, and worship.

The questions around budget and faculty reflect the efforts at balance in the working agreement between Bexley Hall being fully incorporated into CRCDS, but maintaining an Episcopal/Anglican identity within that structure. There was a single budget, developed by CRCDS; the dean of Bexley Hall could advocate for various initiatives or needs but in the end did not have any fiscal authority. If Bexley felt it needed a faculty or staff member, it needed to advocate for that through the centralized budgeting process; if the request was not met, there was little Bexley could do.

We can see how these issues played out with regard to spiritual formation. The Bexley faculty had advocated for resources for spiritual formation and development for students, including student and faculty retreats and more offerings in liturgy and spirituality. Resources were not forthcoming from CRCDS—as a low church, largely Baptist, Bible-and-preaching focused seminary, this simply was not as much of a focus as it was for Episcopal/Anglican students. One of the few resources Bexley did have control over was restricted endowments that the seminary received as part of the separation from Kenyon in 1968. It was precisely these restricted endowment funds, where Bexley did have financial oversight, that were tapped to help fund and organize community retreats and other spiritual formation efforts.[11]

There was a similar issue with regard to the library and library resources. Bexley Hall brought to Rochester a number of library resources as well a small but impressive rare book and manuscript collection and important archival materials. The joint

---

11. Interview with William Petersen, March 13, 2024.

agreement called for a single library with a single collection; Bexley books would be shelved with CRCDS materials but given an additional distinctive marker to designate them as Bexley's. Bexley Hall could request ongoing purchase of materials for the library through the unified budget and could incorporate additional materials acquired through use of separate, restricted Bexley Hall funds. Any additional materials purchased solely by Bexley Hall through its own funds were to remain the property of Bexley Hall. Yet when Bexley would eventually withdraw from the partnership with CRCDS, it was discovered that records were never kept as to which materials had been purchased by Bexley, so nearly all materials acquired post-1968 remained with CRCDS.

Tensions around worship were also consistently noted by nearly all faculty and students interviewed for this project. These tensions, in part, reflect some fundamental differences between a historically and predominantly Baptist institution and an Episcopal/Anglican seminary. Bexley, for one, simply had more worship opportunities: a weekly eucharistic service in addition to a full round of the Daily Offices, as well as commemoration of the liturgical calendar. Bexley was not trying to create a separate or parallel worshiping community. These worship services were open to all students and faculty and were clearly labeled as CRCDS worship services. Yet longstanding tensions persisted; one CRCDS president specifically told the Bexley dean no services could be referred to or labeled as "liturgies" in any public or official seminary communications. According to Bexley faculty and students, CRCDS faculty shared on more than one occasion the concern that these worship services would induce students to convert to The Episcopal Church. These concerns were heightened when Johannes van den Blink, a Presbyterian member of the CRCDS faculty, joined The Episcopal Church, was ordained a priest, and affiliated with the Bexley Hall faculty. This has been characterized by students and faculty from the Rochester years as "causing a stir" to "causing some CRCDS faculty to freak out."[12]

12. Interviews with William Petersen, March 13, 2024; and Richard Hamlin, March 10, 2024.

By the 1990s, these unresolved issues resulted in the reshaping of the cluster, as CRCDS operated for years with systemic, ongoing deficits. Bexley Hall was not alone in feeling the effects of CRCDS's budget issues. St. Bernard's Institute would cease to be an affiliate member of the Rochester theological consortium and would move out of its location on the CRCDS campus, essentially resuming its independent existence. Beginning in 1996, the Bexley Hall board of trustees formed a task force to examine the future of the seminary. In 1997, the board made the decision to formally separate from CRCDS, retain its own accreditation and grant its own degrees, while continuing to remain on the CRCDS campus, to use the CRCDS facilities, and to have its students fulfill degree requirements through courses taken at CRCDS (e.g., biblical studies).[13]

In addition to ending the formal partnership with CRCDS, Bexley Hall also opened an extension site on the campus of Trinity Lutheran Seminary in Columbus, Ohio. This development was a direct result of the ongoing ecumenical dialogues between the Evangelical Lutheran Church in America and The Episcopal Church. Lutheran-Episcopal dialogues had begun in the late 1960s and made steady progress toward theological agreement. In 1997, an initial proposal was presented to both the Churchwide Assembly of the ELCA and the General Convention of The Episcopal Church to establish full communion, including interchangeability of pastors and priests. The Episcopal Church would approve this agreement, which would be narrowly defeated in the Churchwide Assembly of the ELCA. In 1999, the ELCA approved a revised version of the agreement, which The Episcopal Church in turn adopted at its 2000 General Convention. The Rev. Dr. William Petersen, dean of Bexley Hall from 1984–1996, and who continued as a faculty member after leaving the dean's office, served on the Lutheran-Episcopal dialogue alongside the Rev. Dr. Walter Bouman, professor of systematic theology at Trinity Lutheran Seminary. The

---

13. Association of Theological Schools, "Report of a Comprehensive Visit to Bexley Hall Seminary, March 17–20, 2003," 2, Bexley Seabury Seminary Federation Archives.

agreement for full communion included a commitment for both communions to "study one another's basic documents"[14] and a commitment from both communions to collaborate across all levels. This partnership with Trinity reflected not only the burgeoning arrangements between the ELCA and The Episcopal Church and the personal relationships between Bouman and Petersen, but that continued commitment to formation in an ecumenical setting that had marked Bexley Hall for nearly thirty years by that point.

From 1997 to 2008, Bexley Hall operated with two campuses: one in Rochester in collaboration with CRCDS and one in Columbus in collaboration with Trinity Lutheran Seminary. Bexley had reclaimed its own independent accreditation with the Association of Theological Schools, albeit an accreditation "by virtue of partnership" with Trinity and CRCDS. "By virtue of partnership" was necessary for Bexley's accreditation because students took nearly half their courses at either CRCDS or Trinity, since Bexley did not have faculty in several academic areas, focusing on the Episcopal/Anglican elements of the curriculum.

In 2008, the board of trustees decided to close the Rochester site completely and focus all operations at the Columbus campus. There were several factors that contributed to this decision. CRCDS continued to struggle with financial shortfalls and was eliminating faculty and staff positions, leading to concerns as to whether this was a sustainable partnership long term. There were increased demands placed on faculty by having two campuses. Faculty taught in-person courses at two different campus locations (located a five-and-a-half-hour drive from one another). This necessitated either commuting from one campus to another or taking up residence for a semester—in addition to the ongoing collaborative partnership in West Virginia, which required faculty to commute for weekend intensive courses.

A more positive reason for closing the Rochester location was that the Columbus campus proved to be a vibrant, collaborative partnership. Enrollment quickly grew, so that by 2008 there were more students enrolled in Columbus than in Rochester. Bexley

14. Lutheran-Episcopal Dialogue, "Called to Common Mission," para. 4.

was able to reconnect and build upon its historic relationships with the Dioceses of Ohio and Southern Ohio, both of which initially provided financial support to help the satellite campus be established. Cooperation was smoother with Trinity due to the commitments laid out in the full communion proposal, along with greater similarities in theology and liturgy between the ELCA and The Episcopal Church than with a historically Baptist ecosystem. There had been some opposition to the full communion proposal within the ELCA. The initial proposal, the Concordat of Agreement in 1997, did not receive the required two-thirds vote in the Churchwide Assembly, and while the revised proposal, Called to Common Mission, did receive a two-thirds majority at the 1999 ELCA Churchwide Assembly, just over 30 percent of the voting members voted against the proposal. Of the ELCA seminaries, Trinity had been largely in favor of full communion, with Walter Bouman, the systematic theology professor, one of the chief drafters and proponents of Called to Common Mission. While there were some Trinity faculty and supporting synods that had not been in favor of the agreement, these were small minorities among the Trinity community.

Students enrolled in the MDiv program at the Columbus site took roughly half the courses through Trinity Lutheran Seminary, largely in biblical studies, some church history courses, and pastoral care/pastoral theology, with liturgy, theology, and some of the church history requirements provided by the Bexley faculty. Faculty partnerships were collegial and collaborative, with Bexley faculty participating in both Trinity Lutheran faculty meetings and smaller departmental gatherings. Bexley Hall also became a member of the Theological Consortium of Greater Columbus (TCGC), which included Trinity Lutheran Seminary as well as the Methodist Theological School in Ohio and the Roman Catholic seminary, the Pontifical College Josephinum. The TCGC held regular faculty gatherings and an annual lecture series and allowed for students to take courses at other member institutions through cross-registration. Student enrollment made Bexley Hall during this period one of the smallest Episcopal seminaries, with total enrollment averaging between fifteen and twenty students. Students were a mixture of commuters and residential students, drawn mostly but not entirely from Ohio, southern Ohio, western New York, West Virginia, Kentucky, and Lexington. Faculty also remained small, with between three to five faculty members.

Bexley Hall operated out of Bexley House, a residence adjacent to the main Trinity Lutheran campus, which had office space for faculty and support staff, a kitchen, small prayer chapel, and common lounge for students to gather. Of particular importance during the Columbus years was a weekly meal offered by Bexley as a community-building opportunity, Common Meal, which was attended by both Bexley and Trinity students, as well as some faculty and staff. There was a vibrant and common worship life. Trinity Lutheran held daily chapel gatherings, including a weekly celebration of Holy Communion, with Bexley students sharing in assisting at these liturgies and with Bexley faculty assisting in presiding and preaching. The main community weekly Eucharist in the Trinity chapel was celebrated monthly according to an approved liturgy of The Episcopal Church. The Daily Office was prayed, either in a smaller prayer chapel on the Trinity campus or in the worship space in Bexley House. One to two additional eucharistic services were celebrated weekly according to an approved Episcopal Church liturgy. All worship offered was considered to be a common worship experience, not a "Trinity" worship service or a "Bexley" worship service, and both communities regularly ensured participation by both Bexley and Trinity students, staff, and faculty in worship.

By the fall of 2011, however, the seminary was at a turning point. Enrollment had decreased, in part reflecting the overall downturn across The Episcopal Church.[15] The establishment of new Anglican studies programs at schools such as Brite Divinity School, Candler School of Theology at Emory, and Iliff School of Theology, among others, provided increased competition for

---

15. Ordinations across The Episcopal Church were in the 250–270 range in the early 1990s, peaked to around 400 by 1999–2000, to decrease back to 250–270 by the late 2000s.

students, along with the establishment of new, non-accredited training programs such as the Kemper School of Theology in Kansas. Whereas in the 1970s and 1980s nearly 70–75 percent of Episcopal clergy had attended an Episcopal seminary, by the late 2000s that percentage had dropped to barely over 50 percent. Due to financial constraints, the seminary had decreased its number of faculty to three, which was below the threshold for standards set by the Association of Theological Schools for sustainability.[16]

Trinity Lutheran Seminary was also going through its own processes of discernment concerning its future. The issue of declining enrollment was prevalent through seminary education at this time and was not solely confined to The Episcopal Church. Trinity's enrollment dropped nearly by half from 2000 to 2012 as it also weathered the stress of the 2008 financial crisis, which struck endowment-dependent institutions particularly hard. Several ELCA seminaries would begin processes of combining with other seminaries. Gettysburg Seminary and the Lutheran Theological School at Philadelphia would eventually merge to form United Lutheran Seminary, while Lutheran Theological Southern Seminary would become part of Lenoir-Rhyne University, and the Pacific Lutheran Theological Seminary would become part of California Lutheran University. Conversations about possible merger or a more collaborative partnership with the Methodist Theological Seminary were discussed but did not advance to any substantive discussions. Trinity was discerning whether to continue as a stand-alone seminary, consider closer partnership with neighboring Capital University,[17] or explore deeper partnerships with another seminary.

16. Matthew Price, presentation to Council of Deans of the Seminaries of the Episcopal Church, January 11, 2012.

17. Trinity Lutheran Seminary was formed as a merger of two seminaries that had previously been part of Lutheran institutions of higher education. Hamma School of Theology was originally founded in 1845 as part of Wittenberg University in Springfield, Ohio, about an hour west of Columbus. The Evangelical Lutheran Theological Seminary (ELTS) was founded in 1830 and was eventually part of Lutheran-affiliated Capital University before becoming a stand-alone seminary in the 1960s. Hamma and ELTS would merge in

In the interests of full disclosure, it was in the summer of 2011 when I was called as dean of Bexley Hall Seminary. The board of trustees was well aware of the challenges the seminary faced in terms of enrollments and finances, and there were three possible options we discussed for the future.

One was to cease to be a degree-granting institution and fully merge with another school, most likely Trinity Lutheran Seminary given the close working relationship already in place. Another was to try to continue to exist as an independent seminary, accredited by virtue of partnership with Trinity Lutheran. A third option was to explore a collaborative partnership with another Episcopal seminary, with Seabury-Western Theological Seminary the most likely candidate, who had been going through their own period of change and transition—to which we now turn.

1978 to form Trinity Lutheran Seminary, located on the campus of ELTS in Columbus, with ELTS in turn surrounded by the Capital University campus.

CHAPTER 4

Seabury-Western Theological Seminary, 1933–2012

IN THE FALL OF 1933,[1] the newly created Seabury-Western Theological Seminary began instruction with an enrollment of roughly seventy-five students.[2] The new institution was undergoing a threefold process of adjustment. Firstly, Seabury-Western was dealing with the challenge that faces all seminary mergers: of blending two faculties, boards of trustees, student bodies, and institutional histories and cultures. And it was doing so while re-establishing itself in a new location; keep in mind that Western Seminary had not functioned from 1923 to 1928 and had only just moved into the first of its new Evanston campus buildings prior to the merger. During that 1923–1928 period the Western Seminary faculty served in local parishes and the seminary leadership raised funds for its new campus, had to appeal all the way to the Illinois Supreme Court (twice!) to get it built, and then temporarily was located at St. Mark's Church in Evanston while the first campus buildings were under construction. They were not only building the plane while they were flying it, to use a common metaphor.

1. This chapter is the longest in this history, for two main reasons. For one, it covers a longer period of history—1933 to 2012—than the prior chapter. In addition, Seabury-Western has a more fulsome archival record, with greater recourse in this chapter on primary sources.

2. Johnson, "History," 10.

They were rebuilding the interior of the plane at the same time as they were building it while flying it. And, thirdly, all of this was occurring in institutions that were endowment-dependent in the midst of the Great Depression and the financial impact that had not only on American churches, but on higher education in general.

Of the various elements that needed to be sorted out as part of the seminary merger, the question of merging two faculties seemed to be the least fraught. This was due largely to the fact that both seminaries were understaffed at the time of the merger. Seabury Divinity School had been undergoing several years of significant deficit spending and had been in a kind of holding pattern while determining the seminary's future, with the warden and nearly all the faculty above the mandatory resignation age. From the Western side, given the hiatus of the 1920s, when the seminary had ceased to operate, there were several faculty vacancies they were looking to fill as the seminary ramped up operations again.[3] A combined board of trustees began meeting in the fall of 1933, with the bishops of Chicago and Minnesota as ex-officio members, with designated slots for trustees from the Dioceses of Minnesota and Chicago as well as at-large trustee representation. A major factor in helping bring together the two dioceses and faculty was the presence of Bishop Frank McElwain. Bishop McElwain had been a professor and warden of Seabury Divinity School before being elected bishop of Minnesota in 1917. He continued to teach at the seminary during his time as bishop. Stephen Keeler was elected bishop coadjutor of Minnesota in 1931. In part due to financial challenges resulting from the Great Depression, Bishop Keeler, though technically coadjutor, in effect functioned as diocesan bishop, while Bishop McElwain transitioned to a non-stipendiary status and mostly taught at Bishop Seabury Divinity School. Bishop McElwain's support of the merger was crucial to its approval by the Diocese of Minnesota, and he would move to Evanston and continue to teach, eventually serving as dean (while still providing occasional episcopal ministry in Minnesota).

3. Johnson, "History," 2.

Creating a new institutional culture would take more time. A longtime Seabury-Western faculty member said that after the merger "it would take a decade for the chapel wars to be resolved," indicating differences between the more low church Diocese of Minnesota and high church Diocese of Chicago (though always keeping in mind that neither diocese was a monolith).[4] While issues in the chapel might have been resolved within a decade, tensions between advocates of differing church parties would continue well into the 1940s, as we will see. There were also differing perceptions of social class between what was perceived as the generally more rural Diocese of Minnesota and more urban Diocese of Chicago.[5] Russell Johnson, from the Diocese of Minnesota, was a member of the first-year class in the fall of 1933. In his unpublished history of Seabury-Western, he quotes the third-year student who was president of the student body as saying to him when he arrived on campus in Chicago: "We were expecting to greet a bunch of unsophisticated hayseeds, but to our surprise suave, sophisticated men with real class came."[6] In fairness, Johnson also notes that despite this comment, he personally did not experience any kind of slights from his classmates and said that the students rather quickly found a common sense of community.

In the midst of all of these changes, the seminary was also dealing with the financial crisis of the Great Depression. It had been these financial challenges that helped push Seabury Divinity School toward merger, as the trustees realized they would not be able to raise the amount needed for either option considered in the late 1920s/early 1930s, to either renovate the current campus or construct new buildings at Carleton College. These financial challenges were compounded by the impact of the Depression. A significant portion of Bishop Seabury's endowment was impacted by real estate foreclosures, while important components of Western Seminary's income was based on rental income from

---

4. Interview with Newland Smith, April 16, 2024.

5. As with high church and low church matters, both dioceses, in reality, contained both urban and rural parishes and constituencies.

6. Johnson, "History," 11.

commercial property that had suffered greatly in the Depression. At one point in the mid-1930s, the taxes on the commercial real estate held by Seabury-Western exceeded any income derived.[7] It was only through a sense of shared sacrifice that the new seminary was able to survive: the faculty would take a salary cut, Bishop McElwain would eventually serve on the faculty while retired and supported by his pension; and tasks formerly filled by hired staff such as housekeeping and groundskeeping would instead be done by students on a volunteer basis. Eventually Dean Frederick Grant, a major proponent of the merger, would depart in 1937 to become dean of Union Seminary in New York. Bishop McElwain would be called as dean, agreeing to serve through 1944.

After weathering all of these challenges in the 1930s, the seminary would then be faced with the upheavals brought about by World War II. Recall that Bexley Hall vacated the campus and was housed at Virginia Seminary during World War II, due to the combination of declining seminary enrollments due to military service and the need for additional housing on college campuses for officer training. Seabury-Western would continue to operate on its campus, albeit in very different circumstances. Student enrollment would drop by nearly half, and the seminary would reduce its footprint to accommodate the need for additional housing for officer training candidates.[8]

The differences in theology, liturgy, and cultures between the two sponsoring dioceses would reemerge with the search for a new dean to succeed Bishop McElwain. The bishops of each diocese—Bishop Stephen Keeler of Minnesota and Bishop Wallace Conkling of Chicago—served as ex-officio members of the board and each nominated, in essence, their own candidate. Bishop Keeler's nominee was a low church evangelical who was dean of the cathedral in Faribault, Vesper Ward. Bishop Conkling nominated Bernard Iddings Bell, one of the more prominent Anglo-Catholic voices in The Episcopal Church at the time. Neither candidate would be acceptable to the other diocese's contingents on the board of trustees,

7. Johnson, "History," 15–16.
8. Johnson, "History," 17–18.

leading to the decision to call a compromise candidate, Alden Kelley, who at the time of his election in 1945 was serving as director of College Work on the churchwide denominational staff.

Regarding the controversy around calling the next dean, Johnson stated that "as a Trustee of this period [during the search for a dean to succeed Bishop McElwain], I can attest that meetings were primarily a dialogue between Bishop Conkling and Bishop Keeler with each trying to outmaneuver the other. This continuing conflict eventually reached a point threatening the very life of the seminary."[9] Another bishop on the board, Bishop Lewis Whittemore of Western Michigan, requested a discussion at a board meeting on the question of whether Seabury-Western would be "a partisan seminary, or shall it remain a general seminary?" A resolution to have this discussion at a future board meeting was seconded and approved. The January 1950 board of trustees prepared a statement reaffirming Seabury-Western's "role as a general seminary serving the entire church."[10]

In interviewing persons for this history, a frequent aspect of Seabury-Western that was lifted up by nearly all those interviewed was that its formation is an example of a successful seminary merger. There are certainly aspects of this that resonate. By the 1960s and 1970s, Seabury-Western was consistently the fourth, sometimes the third largest Episcopal seminary in terms of enrollment, and counted a number of prominent alumni. But we also cannot overlook just how fraught the first twenty years of this merger were. In the 1930s, the seminary struggled with reconciling two different faculties, seminary cultures, and boards of trustees while at the same time having to deal with financial crises due to the Great Depression. In the 1940s, operations were severely impacted by World War II. In the late 1940s, recurring tensions

9. Johnson, "History," 20.

10. Johnson, "History," 21. The 1950 board of trustees minutes refer to such a discussion and reference an "Appendix E" as an official statement describing the board's position. Unfortunately, this appendix was not included in the minutes in the Bexley Seabury Seminary Federation Archives, and the quotation here is from Johnson's recounting of the statement as a board member present at the January 1950 meeting.

over high church and low church parties resulted in a protracted and conflicted search for a dean to replace Bishop McElwain.

As the 1950s dawned, Seabury-Western was ready to expand and thrive, but it had taken nearly twenty years to get to that place. The seminary was also aided by the broader situation in the church and in higher education. The Episcopal Church entered a period of expansion in the 1950s and 1960s, and seminary enrollments and ordinations increased dramatically. In a prior chapter, we saw how Bexley Hall's enrollment surged from a handful of total students in any given year in the 1940s to enrollments of fifty or more students by the 1960s. Seabury-Western rode the same wave, fortuitously addressing some of its longstanding issues around its merger by the time this surge began in the 1950s.

Charles Harris succeeded Alden Kelley as dean in 1956, and Seabury-Western began to enter a period of sustained growth and expansion. Reflecting the changing nature of seminary enrollments, a major goal for the seminary was to build married student housing in addition to the dormitory that housed single seminarians. In 1950, a majority of seminary students were single; by 1960, nearly a majority were married.[11] In the late 1950s and early 1960s, married student housing and a residence for the dean were both constructed. By the early 1960s, the faculty that had served during the first decades of the merger had gradually been replaced by an entirely new faculty, further blurring the distinctions between who had been primarily connected to "Seabury" and who had been primarily connected to "Western." By the early 1960s, enrollment began to regularly reach one hundred students. Seabury-Western expanded beyond being primarily a midwestern seminary; while there was always a sizable plurality of students from midwestern dioceses, particularly Chicago and Minnesota, increasingly Seabury-Western attracted students from across The Episcopal Church. In 1965, for instance, the entering class of thirty-six students came from thirty-two different dioceses.

It was also in the early 1960s that Seabury-Western admitted its first women students. In the 1930s, there had been a training

11. Johnson, "History," 17.

program for deaconesses in Chicago. Frederick Grant, dean of Seabury-Western, was listed as director of studies for the diocesan deaconess training program, and brochures indicated qualified students would be able to take courses at Seabury-Western. A thorough search of dean's reports, board of trustees minutes, and commencement bulletins did not indicate that any deaconesses ever, in fact, enrolled.[12] By 1939, the training program had been folded into the Philadelphia training center for deaconesses, which did have a cooperative arrangement with the Philadelphia Divinity School. Women training as deaconesses were certainly not foreign to Seabury-Western; the Methodist Church[13] had a large and vibrant deaconess training program that merged in 1934 with Garrett Biblical Institute to form what was then called Garrett Theological Seminary, directly across the street from the Seabury-Western campus. In the 1950s, the Diocese of Chicago had Windham House, a training program for deaconesses. As in the 1930s, there are several mentions in faculty meetings and board of trustees minutes about the possibility of deaconesses in training to take courses at Seabury-Western, but no direct evidence indicating they ever did. Board of trustees minutes indicate conversations about relocating Windham House to the campus of Seabury-Western, and in the late 1950s a team from Windham visited the campus, but the relocation never happened, nor were any deeper or more tangible relationships built between Windham House and Seabury-Western.

The first women to enroll as students in a degree program arrived in the fall of 1961, to the newly created master of arts in Christian education program. The rollout of the MA program and

---

12. This does not mean that there might not have been a handful of deaconesses who enrolled in courses at Seabury-Western, just that the archival record does not provide any confirmation that this did occur. As the common aphorism notes, "absence of evidence is not evidence of absence."

13. The Methodist Church was formed in 1939 through the merger of the Methodist Episcopal Church and the Methodist Episcopal Church, South, the two largest Methodist denominations in the country which had split in 1844 over slavery. In 1968, The Methodist Church would merge with the Evangelical United Brethren to form the current United Methodist Church.

incorporation of women students revealed ingrained resistance to the presence of women at the seminary. One student's recounting of those early years indicated that the admissions letter sent to women students still began with the "Dear Brethren" form letter salutation and asked the student to submit their measurements for a cassock for chapel service, even though women students were not permitted to serve in the chapel. The first classes of women students, during their orientation tour of the seminary, were specifically told they were not permitted to serve on the altar guild; that was reserved for seminarians—despite, as one female student noted, the fact that many of them had served on the altar guild for years before arriving at seminary and continued to do so in the parishes they attended on Sundays in Chicago.[14] The first class of female students were housed at Windham House and were not permitted to take meals in the seminary refectory until housing for female students was available on campus. In contrast to the male seminarians, who did not take many if any courses from Garrett Seminary, the MA in Christian education students took a number of courses through Garrett, since they had a robust Christian education program through their own, long-established deaconess training program.

One of the first female student's personal reflections on those first years indicates that several faculty and a number of students were clearly opposed to the presence of women on campus, but over all a majority of the faculty and seminarians were welcoming. The student in particular recounts the visit of Archbishop Michael Ramsey, who delivered the endowed Hale Lectures in 1959 and returned several years later to receive an honorary degree. During his visit, he held a gathering with the student body, which included the women students in the MA program. As the student recounts,

> We were all attired in our academic gowns which we wore to all classes. After some of my classmates spoke, I raised my hand and was recognized. I asked, "What do you see as the role of women in the church?" His eyes under his

14. Anonymous personal recollection of a female student, Bexley Seabury Seminary Federation Archives.

bushy eyebrows stared at me as he pronounced, "The women should stay in the kitchen." Other questions were voiced, he blessed us, and we adjourned. At that point I found myself surrounded by my brothers, awakened themselves to the rudeness and immediately practicing pastoral care. It was a bewildering moment for me.[15]

Throughout the 1960s, the only women students to be enrolled in a degree-granting program would be in the MA in Christian education, which averaged six to eight students per year and twelve to sixteen total enrollment in the two-year program at any given time at the seminary. The program produced a number of alumni who would later go on to be ordained, such as Phyllis Edwards. Edwards was studying to become a deaconess, graduated from Seabury-Western in 1964, and moved to the Diocese of California. In 1964, Bishop James Pike of the Diocese of California said he considered Edwards to be a deacon and licensed her to serve in the diocese and considered her to be clergy. The dean of Seabury-Western's report to the 1964 board of trustees meeting is dripping with scorn in recounting this event, summarizing it in a single sentence that "the bishop of California threatened to ordain Ms. Edwards to the apostolic ministry."[16]

In 1966, the board of trustees would formally vote to open the bachelor of divinity program to persons not formally in the ordination process. The dean's report to the board of trustees notes that this action reflected the fact that nine out of the eleven seminaries of The Episcopal Church permitted enrollment of persons in the BD program who may not be postulants for Holy Orders.[17] In

---

15. Anonymous personal recollection of a female student, Bexley Seabury Seminary Federation Archives.

16. "Dean's Report to Board of Trustees," Bexley Seabury Seminary Federation Archives.

17. This was also the reason why Bexley Hall never admitted any women students to degree programs during its time in Kenyon. Like a number of Episcopal seminaries, admission to the bachelor of divinity program was restricted to persons who had been admitted as postulants or had permission of their bishops to enroll while pursuing postulancy. Since women by definition could not be admitted as postulants, such policies effectively barred them from

1969, Catherine Owen Welton would be the first woman to graduate with the bachelor of divinity degree, a year before the 1970 General Convention formally approved the ordination of women to the order of deacons and retroactively classified all consecrated deaconesses as ordained deacons.[18] In 1968, Seabury-Western would have its first woman on the board of trustees, Anne Somsen from the Diocese of Minnesota, first appointed to fill out the term of a trustee who resigned, and later elected to a full term. In 1970, a second woman would join the board of trustees, Dr. Jeannette Piccard. Dr. Piccard is a figure of considerable historic importance: in 1918 she received a master's degree in organic chemistry from the University of Chicago and a doctor of education degree from the University of Minnesota in 1942, and for over thirty years she held the record for highest altitude achieved by a woman, as the first woman to enter the stratosphere, through her efforts as a balloonist. She joined the Seabury-Western board in 1970, was ordained a deacon in 1971, and received a certificate of study from General Theological Seminary in 1973. On July 29, 1974, she joined Bexley Hall graduates Merrill Bittner and Betty Bone Scheiss as part of eleven deacons ordained to the priesthood at the Church of the Advocate in Philadelphia, Pennsylvania.

It was also in the early 1970s that Frederica Harris Thompsett joined the faculty as the first tenure-track female faculty member and served on the faculty from 1973 to 1977. Seabury-Western had had female instructors previously. Edith Bideau Normelli was a professionally trained opera singer who had performed across Europe, before beginning in the 1930s to serve as an instructor at Seabury-Western, training students in singing and public speaking. Yet it was clear she was not considered to be in any way on the same scale as the male professors. Sources repeatedly refer to her as "Madame" Bideau Normelli, and in the late 1930s she was a subject of such a humiliating and condescending student parody

---

admission to the bachelor of divinity program.

18. See *Journal of the General Convention of The Episcopal Church* (1970), 249 and 270–71.

skit that the dean demanded a formal apology from the student body to her.[19]

The ordinations in Philadelphia in 1974 placed institutions of The Episcopal Church in the place of having to determine whether to permit those ordained as priests to preside at the sacraments or whether to postpone such a decision until after the 1976 General Convention would address the matter. There is no indication in the written record that Bexley Hall restricted the participation of the ministry of the clergy ordained in July of 1974, though there is also no direct evidence found during the course of this study that determined if any of those ordained did preside at any of Bexley Hall's worship services between 1974 and 1976. Seabury-Western was in a different situation: Bishop James Montgomery of the Diocese of Chicago opposed the ordination of women and stated he would not permit any of those ordained in July of 1974 to preside at the sacraments in the Diocese of Chicago. After the ordination of women to the priesthood was approved in 1976, Bishop Montgomery would permit women to be ordained in the Diocese of Chicago, but he declined to do so himself, and Suffragan Bishop Quintin Primo would preside at ordination of women in the diocese until the election of Bishop Frank Griswold in 1987. Bishop Philip McNairy of the Diocese of Minnesota, on the other hand, was a firm supporter of the ordination of women to the priesthood, and it was through his diocese's allotment on the board of trustees that the first two women trustees joined the board. After the ordinations of the Philadelphia Eleven in July 1974 the Seabury-Western board of trustees issued a formal letter of censure to the Rev. Dr. Jeanette Piccard, stating, in part, "It is the policy of this Board to remain faithful to the Constitution and Canons of The Episcopal Church and to the proper Ecclesiastical authority as the invitations are extended to those who will function or celebrate officially at the Eucharist at Seabury-Western Theological Seminary."[20] Thus Seabury-Western not only formally censured

---

19. Johnson, "History," 13–14.

20. Minutes of the Board of Trustees, October 1974; Bexley Seabury Seminary Federation Archives.

Jeanette Piccard, but also formally adopted the policy that the clergy ordained in July of 1974 would not be permitted to preside at the sacraments in the seminary chapel. An additional member of the Philadelphia Eleven, Alla Bozarth Campbell, also had Seabury connections. Bozarth Campbell received bachelor's, master's and PhD degrees from Northwestern University. Records indicate she did not enroll in a degree program at Seabury-Western, but she did take several classes while independently reading for orders to complete canonical requirements for ordination.

Contemporary seminary newsletters and dean's reports indicate that the faculty and the student body were supporters of the ordination of women. Just days before the 1976 General Convention was to gather, Dean O. C. Edwards sent a letter to the seminary community on behalf of the faculty that specifically stated, and listed by name, that nine out of the ten current faculty members supported the ordination of women, and that while one faculty member hoped that General Convention "will not" approve the ordination of women, that faculty member nevertheless "will abide by its [General Convention's]" decision.[21] There would continue to be tension on the board of trustees, however.

At its October 1977 meeting the House of Bishops addressed the decisions taken at the 1976 General Convention. Presiding Bishop John Allin stated that he did not think women could be priests any more than they could be husbands or fathers and offered to resign. Bishop Allin was persuaded by the other bishops to stay on as presiding bishop, and the House of Bishops adopted a conscience clause, stating that "No Bishop, Priest, or Lay Person should be coerced or penalized in any manner, not suffer any canonical disabilities as a result of his or her conscientious objection to or support of the sixty-fifth General Convention's actions with regard to the ordination of women to the priesthood or episcopate."[22] The conscience clause was adopted by the House of Bishops only during its regular meeting in between gatherings of

---

21. Letter from O. C. Edwards to Seabury-Western Seminary community, September 9, 1976; Bexley Seabury Seminary Federation Archives.
22. An Episcopal Glossary of the Church, "Conscience Clause."

General Convention, and never by the House of Deputies, so it had no official standing of any kind. Yet supporters of women's ordination raised concerns it would allow for bishops and dioceses not to implement the ordination of women to the priesthood. Which is indeed what happened: well into the 1990s, there would be dioceses that would not permit the ordination of women nor permit women to serve as priests.[23]

At the October 1977 Seabury-Western board of trustees meeting, held barely days after the House of Bishops meeting, a resolution was proposed that the seminary formally adopt this conscience clause as seminary policy. Anne Somsen, the first woman to serve on the board and a member since 1968, objected to this proposed resolution. On grounds of process, she said they did not even have the full text of the action that the House of Bishops had adopted that they were voting on to be seminary policy. In terms of the statement itself, she said that it would indicate that Seabury-Western was not fully supportive of women in ordained ministry. The resolution passed, and, in protest, Somsen resigned from the board. In her resignation letter she indicated she was still "committed to the support of theological education, but only when such education is available to all members of the church" and that "I want no part of an official statement which allows bishops, priests, deacons and laymen to deny a canon of the church with impunity."[24] Regarding the responsibility to uphold the Constitution and Canons, she further noted that "I find it inconsistent to send a letter of censure to Jeanette Piccard but not to John Allin to remain faithful to the Canons"[25] given that

---

23. It would not be until 1997 that the General Convention would formally end this practice, changing the Constitution and Canons to forbid dioceses to exclude women from the ordination process, or deny women a license to officiate or serve in a diocese, based solely on gender. See Resolution A053 of the 1997 General Convention: General Convention, *Journal*, 112.

24. Anne Somsen, letter to Dean O. C. Edwards, November 16, 1977; Bexley Seabury Seminary Federation Archives.

25. Somsen, letter to Bishop James Montgomery, Chair of the Seabury-Western Board, October 20, 1977; Bexley Seabury Seminary Federation Archives.

the General Convention had formally approved the ordination of women as priests and deacons. The members of the board of trustees with Minnesota connections would later write a letter of support of Anne Somsen's resignation, stating that they "share completely Anne Somsen's displeasure" and that "we do not see the issue at hand as being women's ordination. The issue is whether the members of the Board of Trustees can and will truly respect differences of opinion on these or any other subjects . . . . We see the need for serious effort toward reconciliation—not of opinions but of persons."[26]

In his responses, Dean O. C. Edwards expressed his own regret, saying that he felt "bereft." Trying to walk a middle ground, he noted that the overwhelming majority of the faculty had been very clear about their support of women's ordination, an increase in the number of women students, and that his interpretation of the board's action was to spell out "what was already the case: Seabury-Western has as one of its most abiding traditions the desire to comprehend all of the traditions within the Episcopal Church." Yet in the same letter he notes that Frederica Thompsett, the only female tenure-track faculty member, would be leaving the seminary after only four years.[27]

Another snapshot of the role of women at Seabury-Western comes from a 1985 response to a survey being conducted concerning Episcopal seminaries' engagement with women in ministry. Seabury-Western's response to the survey notes that there is a course offered on women in ministry . . . yet it was taught on a biennial basis by a full-time male faculty member and an adjunct female faculty member. The response further notes that the seminary faculty is "an exclusively male faculty, except for occasional adjunct faculty members," and that women priests from

---

26. Letter from S. Barry O'Leary, on behalf of Minnesota members of the Board of Trustees, to the entire Board of Trustees, December 16, 1977; Bexley Seabury Seminary Federation Archives.

27. Letter from O.C. Edward to Anne Somsen, November 28, 1977; Bexley Seabury Seminary Federation Archives.

the broader church are regularly invited to preach and preside at eucharistic services. The response also acknowledges

> Our student body includes students whose dioceses do not yet accept female candidates for Holy Orders, and who personally may have convictions either that women cannot theologically receive Holy Orders, or that it is not at present appropriate they do so. Our policy is not to attempt to change the convictions of such students, but rather to encourage open dialogue on the issues involved. Many do change their opinions during their seminary years.[28]

While the number of women students would show a steady, gradual increase through the 1980s, it would not be until the early 1990s that there would be another tenure-track female faculty member.

In the mid-1980s, Seabury-Western would embark on another initiative: providing comprehensive theological education and formation for Native Americans preparing for ministry in The Episcopal Church. Seabury-Western, as noted in chapter 3, had had prior engagement with providing education and formation for Native Americans. Enmegahbowh, the first Native American to be ordained in The Episcopal Church, was part of James Lloyd Breck's missionary work. Although Breck baptized and tutored Enmegahbowh, it is a bit anachronistic, if not a bit triumphalist, to claim that this was "the beginning of Seabury Divinity School."[29] As noted in chapter 2, Breck did envision a school for Native Americans to be part of the suite of educational institutions to be founded in Faribault, and one operated briefly before closing.

In 1880, Sherman Coolidge would enroll at Seabury Divinity School and graduate with the degree of bachelor of divinity in 1884, making him the first Native American to earn a BD degree from an Episcopal seminary. The original student registry book

---

28. William Haugaard, Associate Dean for Academic Affairs, letter to Rev. Professor Wilson-Kastner, February 7, 1985; Bexley Seabury Seminary Federation Archives.

29. "The Role of Seabury-Western in the Theological Education of Native Americans," 1991; Bexley Seabury Seminary Federation Archives.

from Seabury Divinity School lists all of Coolidge's personal information—date of birth, baptism, enrollment, admission to postulancy and candidacy, dates ordained, and other data. The book also has a final column under the heading "Remarks," which often serves as a kind of alumni record, where students' placements throughout their careers are updated and noted. For Coolidge, that column reads: "Full blooded Arapahoe Indian. Deacon June 14, 1884, Bishop Whipple. Active in Indian Leadership. Honorary Canon of St. John's, Denver. Died January 24, 1932."[30] For what it is worth, in the original entry, "Arapahoe" was spelled incorrectly, and was later corrected by a different hand.

It would be nearly fifty years before another Native American would graduate. Harold Jones was a Santee Sioux born in Mitchell, South Dakota. He was raised by his grandparents, the Rev. William Holmes, an Episcopal priest and native Santee, and Rebecca, of Caucasian descent. Jones would be offered a full scholarship by the Diocese of Minnesota to attend Seabury-Western, where he enrolled in the fall of 1935. Jones recounts, overall, being accepted by his fellow students, though not without the unchallenged, casual racism endemic at the time.[31] He insisted on being treated the same as the other students; for example, the dean recommended he not take Greek, since he had not had any prior study in other languages. But Jones insisted on taking Greek since the majority of the other white students did so. A major resource for Jones was Bishop McElwain, former bishop of Minnesota who had ministered to Native American communities. Jones notes with surprised awe that McElwain could offer feedback on sermons Jones preached in his native Santee.[32] Jones would eventually be elected seminary president for this third and senior year.

---

30. Student register, Seabury Divinity School; Bexley Seabury Seminary Federation Archives. For a fuller description of Sherman Coolidge's ministry, see Anderson, *400 Years*, 225 and 228–29.

31. Jones recounts his classmates encouraging him to get involved in a seminary activity by saying, "Don't be such a cigar store Indian." See Cochran, *Dakota Cross Bearer*, 79.

32. Cochran, *Dakota Cross Bearer*, 92–93.

Jones also experienced systemic racism in the broader Chicago community. He recounts repeatedly being asked to speak at other churches, both Episcopal and non-Episcopal, to talk about his life. He notes the anger and humiliation he felt looking at flyers that advertised his talks as "Come See a Live Indian." He also notes the shock he felt when, in other contexts, he was treated as white. He shares a story about going to a jazz club with one of the students enrolled from China and was informed by the doorman that he could be admitted, but his friend could not, being told: "Indians are welcome, but Chinks are not."[33]

The seminary was also eventually caught in the middle in the conflict between Jones and his sponsoring diocese. The presenting incident was his election as class president. The news made the rounds of Episcopal Church media and would eventually be picked up by broader wire services. Jones recounts meeting with Dean Grant, who shared a letter he had received from the diocese, which accused the seminary of "pampering" and "spoiling" Jones, and expressed displeasure with the additional speaking opportunities at local churches he had done. After not communicating with him at all for two years, the diocesan examining chaplains announced in this letter to the dean that he would need to return to South Dakota, where they would assess what he had learned, "to satisfy ourselves his time with you [Grant] has not been wasted."[34]

In his meeting with the examining chaplains that summer, Jones recounts that not only was it a confrontational encounter; it was patently unfair. They asked him about material he had not yet covered in his coursework, resulting in him returning for his senior year with a letter to Dean Grant telling Jones to "study and forget the frills" and another warning not to pamper or spoil Jones.[35] Jones would eventually be summoned back to the diocese as the end of his senior year in seminary approached, with the diocesan Board of Examining Chaplains insisting he sit for another round of canonical examinations before the semester ended. Since this

---

33. Cochran, *Dakota Cross Bearer*, 89.
34. Cochran, *Dakota Cross Bearer*, 93.
35. Cochran, *Dakota Cross Bearer*, 101.

meant he would be unable to complete the seminary's own graduation comprehensive examinations, Jones was informed with great regret by Dean Grant he would not be able to receive the bachelor of divinity degree, but would be able to receive a licentiate certificate.[36] Dean Grant offered to let Jones sit for his seminary exams at a later date and expressed the desire to be as flexible as possible in trying to help him complete the degree requirements, but Jones had concerns about how this would be financially possible and whether he would have the time to study after ordination and beginning ministry. Summoned to return to sit for canonical examinations, Jones left Seabury-Western six days before commencement. After being elected suffragan bishop in South Dakota and becoming the first Native American to serve as bishop, he would be awarded an honorary degree in 1972.

The 1960s saw the creation in The Episcopal Church of the National Committee on Indian Work (NCIW) and the eventual appointment of a churchwide staff officer. Another Native American priest, Lester Kills Crow, would attend and graduate from Seabury-Western in 1965. The 1967 General Convention Special Program provided a grant to Cook Theological School in Tempe, Arizona, which was part of a broader outreach ministry of the Presbyterian Church. Throughout the 1970s there would be sporadic funding and grants to Cook, and roughly twenty Episcopalians would be involved in training and formation through the school.[37] In the 1970s and 1980s, training efforts for Native Americans would start to become concentrated in the Native American

---

36. Until canonical revisions in the early 1970s created the General Board of Examining Chaplains and the General Ordination Examinations, there was no centralized, churchwide process for determining competencies in areas of theological education and formation. Each diocese had its own process determined by its own Board of Examining Chaplains, and each seminary had its own version of canonical examinations. Since approval for ordination was determined at the diocesan level, it was not unusual for students not to receive the bachelor of divinity degree and to receive a certificate or other summary of material covered.

37. See Anderson, *400 Years*, 292.

Theological Association (NATA).[38] This was an ecumenical consortium involving Lutherans, Presbyterians, Methodists, the United Church of Christ, and The Episcopal Church, which provided significant funding. NATA offered courses and trainings that Native American candidates for ministry could combine with study at other seminaries. For a time the Rev. Steven Charleston served as both executive director of the NCIW and as chair of the board of NATA, and from 1978 to 1985, six Native American Episcopalians who had been formed through NATA were ordained.[39] In the mid-1980s, there were initial discussions about whether Seabury-Western could partner with NATA to provide some instruction and to offer academic credit to courses offered by NATA through its accreditation by the Association of Theological Schools.

These conversations were shaped by NATA's looming financial insolvency, due in large part to sporadic and inconsistent funding from its sponsoring denominations. With the funding challenges NATA was facing, conversations between the NCIW and Seabury-Western took a different direction, with the eventual establishment of the Evanston Covenant. The Covenant involved representatives from Seabury-Western, the NCIW, NATA, and other leaders in The Episcopal Church. It acknowledged the Church was facing "a leadership crisis confronting The Episcopal Church in its Native American ministry" and called for a "cohesive, consistent, and cooperative response on the national level." It further stated that this response would involve educational models "reflective of and responsive to the unique cultural values and traditions of Native American people" and affirmed that Seabury-Western would be "integral to the development of ordained leadership," along with NATA.[40] The NCIW provided significant funding—nearly sixty thousand dollars per year—as did Venture in Mission (usually abbreviated VIM), a churchwide grant-making program, scholarship funds held by the Episcopal Diocese of Minnesota, and grants

---

38. Anderson, *400 Years*, 322.
39. Anderson, "Native American Seminary Enrollment Increasing."
40. "Evanston Covenant"; Bexley Seabury Seminary Federation Archives.

provided by the Diocese of New Jersey. The goal was to provide full funding for Native American students attending Seabury-Western.

The program operated from 1986 to 1993. Sixteen Native American students attended during that time; eight completed the program and graduated; and four were still serving in Native American congregations by 1996.[41] A participant in the program reflected, in hindsight, "Indian students were set up for failure."[42] A Seabury-Western faculty member at the time wrote that "for most [Native American students] it was a harrowing experience in spite of the commitments and concerns" named in the Evanston Covenant.[43]

The failure of the Evanston Covenant and program from 1986 to 1993 reflects the ways in which systemic racism can shape an institution's failure to engage in a collaborative partnership of equals. Archival records from the period, plus conversations with those who worked on the Evanston Covenant, evidence three overlapping reasons for the failure of the program.

One was the lack of resources provided for Native American students to accommodate to a graduate academic program. As one participant noted, "The average non-Indian student at Seabury-Western at the time was in their early 40s, had a bachelor's degree, and had come from an Anglo congregation. Most of the Indian students did not have a bachelor's degree and came from non-Anglo congregations. The Indian students who had bachelor's degrees and who had more experience in Anglo congregations were generally the ones who were able to complete the program."[44] For some, the transition to an urban, graduate, residential academic setting was a significant academic and cultural shock, and the seminary did not significantly invest in any additional staff or resources, though it did bring onboard a chaplain to Native American students.

A second reason was that Native Americans students were, essentially, shoehorned into what was an overwhelmingly

---

41. Anderson, *400 Years*, 327.
42. Interview with Bradley Hauff, May 24, 2024.
43. Smith, "Doctrine of Discovery Lament Offering 2," para. 4.
44. Interview with Bradley Hauff, May 24, 2024.

Eurocentric curriculum, and no systemic efforts were made to reshape the curriculum to reflect Native American history, theology, or spirituality, despite the commitments named in the Evanston Covenant. Newland Smith again notes: "this institution of the Episcopal Church failed to work with the Native American network to develop a curriculum that was appropriate for its Native American students to navigate its Eurocentric curriculum. The syllabus of one of the courses required of all students, Approaches to the Study of Religion and Theology, included readings by Eliade, Ricoeur, and Tillich. There were no courses, even electives, on Native American history, culture, and spirituality."[45] Eventually an elective on Native American spirituality was added, but the adjunct instructor hired to teach it was a white person of European descent who was a doctoral student at the University of Chicago. All of this was despite the specific naming in the Evanston Covenant of the need for "a flexible [curriculum] design which utilizes all training modes, the local schools, the seminaries, workshops in the field, etc., is needed to meet the varied needs of [Native American] students" and the need to "encourage a truly indigenous Native approach in spirituality and instruction."[46] The very commitments the seminary failed to develop were specifically identified as essential elements before the program even began.

Further, no significant changes or course corrections were made, even though concerns were raised at the time. Owanah Anderson, the staff officer for Native American ministries at the time, along with Bishop Craig Anderson (bishop of South Dakota at the time), and others—including some Seabury-Western faculty—expressed concern about students who had dropped out of the program and the seminary's investment in resources to accommodate Native American students. Eventually the program would be ended, largely because the NCIW and Owanah Anderson would no longer support it. From 1986 to 1991, NCIW had provided

---

45. Smith, "Doctrine of Discovery Lament Offering 2," para. 5.

46. "The Role of Seabury-Western in the Theological Education of Native Americans," internal seminary report, 1991, 3; Bexley Seabury Seminary Federation Archives.

roughly 354,000 dollars in grants to support Native American students—nearly 815,000 dollars adjusted for inflation.[47] Nearly half the students did not complete the program of study, resulting in a legacy of "pain and shame."[48]

In her landmark history of The Episcopal Church's engagement with Native American and Indigenous ministries, Owanah Anderson stated that the effort to have Seabury-Western be designated the seminary for Native American students came to a "dreary conclusion." She was being far, far too kind. The seminary compiled its own internal report and review in 1991, and its assessments are breathtaking in demonstrating a contemporaneous inability to address the institution's failure to provide resources for its Native American students. The report does note that NCIW and Seabury-Western were "not in full communication with each other," yet gives no indication any effort was made by the seminary to work on those communication issues, and then concludes that "it is not surprising, therefore, that a lot of expectations were not met either way." In response to the need for better coordination, NCIW appointed a "Seabury Oversight, Research, and Admissions Advisory Committee" to advocate for Native American students. The report states simply that it did not "know what happened next" with regard to that committee. The report finds ways to declare victory in spite of the program ending with nearly half the students failing to complete the course of study: "When one considers the handicaps . . . the amazing thing is how much got done."[49]

The 1991 report provides a listing of all students who had attended up to that point. Essentially, only biographical information is given, and there is a complete absence of reflection on any role or responsibilities from the seminary or any of its possible failures. To give just one example, the report notes that for one student, "While Seabury was difficult for him academically and

---

47. "Role of Seabury Western," 16; Bexley Seabury Seminary Federation Archives.

48. Interview with Bradley Hauff, May 24, 2024.

49. "Role of Seabury-Western," 4; Bexley Seabury Seminary Federation Archives.

culturally, his work was at least at a minimal level of acceptability and he would have been allowed to return if he had not left school before completing his Spring quarter." The blame in the report for failure to complete the program is uniformly laid entirely on the students, noting with regard to the student mentioned above "he also had a restlessness that appeared to make it hard to stick with any task very long." For another student, the report notes that person "found the curriculum here more demanding than any other Native American student" and that the faculty "recommended that he have no further academic training." This is for a student who already had been ordained a transitional deacon, already had an undergraduate degree, and already had previous graduate study before enrollment—yet the onus is placed entirely on the student's failures.[50]

Another section of the report openly admits the seminary was unprepared for different learning styles. It states concerning one participant that "after he began his work . . . he discovered that he was so completely formed in an oral culture that he could only adapt imperfectly to the world of reading, writing, and abstract thought he found here. While he passed his courses, there was an agreement between him, the diocese, and the seminary that his further preparation would not be pursued most profitably in an extended residential program."[51] Here the different cultural and learning styles are named, but the seminary completely absolves itself and puts the entirety of the blame on the student's failure to adapt.

A final section of the report is focused on "Seminary Learnings from the Covenant Experience." This section does state that "anybody who has been a party to the experience knows that it has not gone well in every case as it could have" and names several issues "needing attention." As in the biographical summaries of students, important issues are named, but the report offers little

50. "Role of Seabury-Western," 9; Bexley Seabury Seminary Federation Archives.

51. "Role of Seabury-Western," 11; Bexley Seabury Seminary Federation Archives.

in way of what could be done differently. It notes that "different students have different needs" and there needs to be a curriculum with "flexible design" but does not offer a single suggestion on what Seabury-Western could have done, or is planning to do (this report is compiled in 1991, with the program still ongoing), but instead calls for national or diocesan guidelines to assist in these areas.[52]

The report does name several of the seminary's failures. One concerns developing channels of communication with students. It notes that "there is a lack of a good system of communication" and that a crucial example of this is "the issue of communication between Indian students and their families at the seminary with both non-Indian students and the administration and faculty." The report further states that the failure of the seminary to "establish regular channels of communication" reflects "iniquities of power that inhibit communication, but also the racism that is never completely eliminated."[53] Elsewhere the report states that the seminary did not develop resources to support a "truly indigenous Native approach to spirituality" and that the seminary had been "actively seeking funds for an Indian faculty member for some time, but so far they have not been forthcoming."[54] It is important that the seminary was able to name its failures in communication and staffing to support the Evanston Covenant; yet in doing so it still offers very little in tangible steps to address those concerns at the very time when the program was still ongoing.

The program at Seabury-Western failed in nearly every aspect laid out in the original Evanston Covenant. The story of the Evanston Covenant, the failure of the program from 1986 to 1993 to provide Native American education and formation, and the lack of accountability named by Seabury-Western have been difficult

---

52. "Role of Seabury-Western," 18–19; Bexley Seabury Seminary Federation Archives.

53. "Role of Seabury-Western," 21; Bexley Seabury Seminary Federation Archives.

54. "Role of Seabury-Western," 22; Bexley Seabury Seminary Federation Archives.

to write. Aware of my own role as an Episcopalian of Anglo and European descent giving an historical overview of the experiences of Native American students, I have attempted to incorporate the perspectives of those involved in the program as much as possible. In personal interviews for this project, I thanked those Native Americans I spoke with for being willing to revisit these traumas in the service of this necessary truth-telling. From the Seabury-Western side, we must clearly state the difference between intention and impact: all sources at the time indicate a sense of hope, excitement, and opportunity in this burgeoning partnership between NCIW and Seabury-Western. Yet despite that, in its official report on the program the seminary repeatedly blamed students for their own failures and takes no responsibility or accountability. The Episcopal Church has been called to name, address, and lament its complicity in the physical and cultural genocide of Native American and Indigenous communities, and the Church has been engaged in processes of lamentation for these actions.[55] This process of self-examination, lament, and truth-telling must continue to be part of these bicentennial celebrations of Bexley Seabury, and if this history is to be anything more than a collection of words, may it be part of continued conversations and tangible actions to address historical injustices.

Going into the 1990s, Seabury-Western carved out a place for itself within the ecosystem of The Episcopal Church and theological education and formation. It continued with important legacy commitments to the broader church with the Hale Lectures and the *Anglican Theological Review*. The Hale Lectures increasingly included ecumenical participants from other traditions along with Episcopal and Anglican scholars, and its collected volumes are important contributions to liturgy, theology, biblical studies, and spirituality. First published in 1918, the *Anglican Theological Review* has continued to be a preeminent scholarly journal in the Anglican and Episcopal world, starting with its very first issue, which published an article from renowned theologian Vida

---

55. A complete set of resources may be found at Episcopal Church Indigenous Ministries, "Doctrine of Discovery Resources."

Dutton Scudder over fifty years before Seabury-Western would hire its first tenure-track female faculty member. In the 1990s, Seabury-Western's role in theological education and formation for the broader Episcopal Church would be further marked by the creation of the Seabury Institute. Dedicated to congregational development, the Institute provided both ongoing continuing education and training for practitioners along with enhancing opportunities for current students.

The number of women students gradually showed an increase. By the mid-1990s, the number of women on the faculty also began to show a gradual increase as well. We get a contemporaneous snapshot of Seabury-Western's identity during this time from a study of all Episcopal seminaries coordinated by Middle Tennessee State University's Office of Communication Research, with the findings presented in a summary report to Seabury-Western. It notes that Seabury-Western is known for being rooted in the Catholic tradition of The Episcopal Church, while also being supportive of women and LGBTQIA+ persons. Yet the report also states that in its surveying of bishops and clergy and lay leaders, Seabury-Western was not necessarily named first or was the first choice for people seeking such a seminary. This led to the report comparing Seabury-Western to Royal Crown Cola: "It would not be unfair to say that Seabury-Western is the RC Cola of Episcopal seminaries. It is among the most popular of soft drinks, the colas; everybody likes it when they try it; but they still think of Coke and Pepsi first when they go to market."[56]

In the 1990s, Seabury-Western gradually became more diverse, with increasing numbers of women among the students and faculty, and was welcoming of LGBTQIA+ persons. The seminary also began to attempt to address its historic rootedness in whiteness by developing programs and opportunities to diversify the seminary community with regard to race. Efforts were made to recruit students of color, and in 1999 the first tenure-track faculty

---

56. "Seabury-Western Theological Seminary Image and Reputational Study," Communication Research Center, Middle Tennessee State University, 1990; Bexley Seabury Seminary Federation Archives.

member of color was added, with Frank Yamada hired to teach Old Testament. A seminary-wide Anti Racism Committee was established, and the entire community—faculty, staff, and students—participated in diversity training. These efforts would continue with the formation of SeaburyNext, which also engaged in community-wide trainings in diversity and anti-racism, and would later be incorporated into the Bexley Seabury Seminary Federation through processes of curricular and institutional formation leading up to reaccreditation in 2015 and 2022. The first tenure-track professor of color, Frank Yamada, would also have the distinction of perhaps having the shortest tenure of a seminary faculty member. The same board of trustees meeting which would later declare exigency—thus allowing the seminary to lay off faculty without regard to tenure—also granted tenure to Yamada. As he noted, "I was a tenured faculty member for 13 minutes and 45 seconds before the Board then voted to end tenure."[57]

Several factors would converge to bring about radical change and restructuring to Seabury-Western in the early 2000s. One of these was persistent, ongoing financial constraints going back decades. This is a common challenge to freestanding denominational seminaries, and not unique to Seabury-Western. Deans' reports and board of trustees minutes dating back to the 1970s noted financial deficits, the need for better fundraising, and concerns about enrollment, and these issues arose time and again throughout the 1980s, 1990s, and 2000s. These persistent financial concerns were, in turn, impacted by broader changes in The Episcopal Church and in higher education. Seminary enrollments among mainline Protestant seminaries overall began to decline in the late 1990s. In The Episcopal Church, this was compounded by the development of diocesan training programs such as the Bishop Kemper School of Theology, as well as the establishment of Anglican studies programs in a number of places, such as Candler School of Theology at Emory and Iliff School of Theology in Denver, among others. As noted in the last chapter, by the early 1990s, nearly 70 percent of persons ordained in The Episcopal Church had attended

---

57. Interview with Frank Yamada, May 1, 2024.

an Episcopal seminary, and by the late 2000s, that number had dropped to roughly 50 percent. These factors are reflected in Seabury-Western's numbers: In the 1960s, Seabury-Western had roughly ninety-five to one hundred students enrolled. By the early 2000s, this was nearly half that, in the fifty to sixty range. Alongside these broader trends, Seabury-Western's financial situation was further shaped by the construction of a new building in the late 1990s/early 2000s, adding space by connecting existing buildings. This was financed mostly through debt, providing further challenges to the seminary's financial outlook. A capital campaign planned in the mid 2000s, in part to address debt incurred by the new building, failed to reach its goals, and the seminary's financial problems were worsened with continuing deferred maintenance on the now nearly seventy-five-year-old campus.[58] An additional factor was that Northwestern University owned the land on which the seminary was located, leasing it to Seabury-Western, while the seminary owned the buildings. This arrangement limited opportunities with regard to any kind of sale or potential redevelopment. This meant options taken at the time, for instance, by Episcopal Divinity School (forming a partnership with Lesley University) or General Theological Seminary (developing part of the campus into for-profit housing) were not possible for Seabury-Western given that Northwestern owned the land.

A special task force was established to look at possible scenarios for the future of Seabury-Western. In February of 2008, the decision was made by the board of trustees to declare financial exigency and to suspend the master of divinity program. Declaring financial exigency allowed the seminary to take steps toward radical restructuring, in part by ending tenure for faculty. Some faculty would be part of the reconfigured institution, while others were given eighteen months to transition to new positions. Seabury-Western reshaped itself as SeaburyNext, focusing on the DMin in congregational development and DMin in preaching through the Association of Chicago Theological Schools (ACTS), providing Anglican studies courses to students enrolled in other

---

58. Interview with Gary Hall, March 1, 2024.

seminaries, and offering education and formation opportunities for all the baptized. The buildings in Evanston were sold to Northwestern University, and SeaburyNext relocated the ELCA Churchwide headquarters located near O'Hare Airport.

At the same time, in the midst of these changes, there were still challenges in developing a sustainable financial model for SeaburyNext. This led in 2009 to the beginnings of joint conversations with Bexley Hall. In 2010, the two schools began holding concurrent board of trustees meetings and appointed a joint committee to look at possibilities of collaborative ministries. In our concluding chapter, we look at the formation of Bexley Seabury Seminary Federation.

CHAPTER 5

Bexley Seabury Seminary Federation, 2012-present

BY THE 2011–2012 ACADEMIC year, both Bexley Hall and SeaburyNext were facing uncertain futures. Bexley was facing financial and enrollment challenges and had an entirely residential seminary formation model at a time when low-residency and online learning were poised to fundamentally impact higher education. SeaburyNext had embraced new models of education and formation but was still struggling with finding a financially viable model to sustain this vision. Both seminaries were also facing an essentially existential question: was there enough capacity in The Episcopal Church for two small seminaries in the Midwest?[1]

A fundamental realization was that both seminaries brought important gifts to a potential new partnership. Bexley Hall brought a focus on preparing people for lay and ordained ministries through its sole degree program, the master of divinity. While Seabury had suspended its MDiv—not eliminated, as sometimes

---

1. There are two other additional seminaries in the Midwest, with Trinity School for Ministry in Pittsburgh and Nashotah House in Wisconsin. Yet these seminaries had carved out a niche within the seminary ecosystem: TSM largely served the conservative, evangelical wing of The Episcopal Church, and Nashotah was committed to the high church, Anglo-Catholic constituency, and neither were generally competing for the same group of students as Bexley Hall and SeaburyNext.

is stated—it did not have the resources after 2008 to offer the degree should it have wanted to do so. SeaburyNext offered courses in Anglican studies, but to offer an MDiv required a broader set of resources: courses in biblical studies, pastoral care, and field education programs. Bexley did have these resources, both on its own and through its accreditation affiliation with Trinity Lutheran Seminary. Bexley also had no outstanding debt or buildings to maintain and had approximately eight million dollars in endowments and restricted assets to bring to a partnership. From its end, SeaburyNext had been a pioneer in developing low-residency and online courses within The Episcopal Church seminary system. It offered residential courses spread over three weekends or in week-long, five-day intensives, online courses with synchronous sessions, and fully online offerings. SeaburyNext had also developed an innovative partnership with the Kellogg School of Management at Northwestern University, where students in the doctor of ministry program in congregational development had access to courses and faculty in leadership and not-for-profit development. Its location at the ELCA Center in Chicago provided a readily accessible hub not only for the seminary community, but for hosting other meetings, conferences, and events for the broader church. SeaburyNext also brought its financial assets, roughly some seventeen million dollars in endowments, to a potential partnership, and likewise had no long-term debt or buildings to maintain.

The two schools also shared some characteristics, most notably a significant common commitment to ecumenical cooperation and collaboration in theological education and formation. Bexley Hall was engaged in the most substantial collaboration in theological education between the ELCA and The Episcopal Church with its joint partnership with Trinity Lutheran Seminary. SeaburyNext was also engaged with the ACTS consortium, not only with cross registration but also with a joint degree program, the doctor of ministry in preaching. Seabury had a longstanding partnership with Garrett Evangelical, including the merging of library resources in a single, common United Library partnership. Each seminary had developed partnerships to offer Anglican studies for

Episcopal students enrolled in other institutions, partnerships that had increased potential as Episcopalians increasingly enrolled in non-Episcopal seminaries. At the time of the discussions around a deeper relationship, SeaburyNext also offered a joint doctor of ministry degree in conjunction with the Church Divinity School of the Pacific.

In addition to bringing gifts and resources to a common venture, the discussions from 2010 to 2012 also looked to the past and to the founding vision for both seminaries. Breck established what became Bishop Seabury Divinity School as part of an effort to establish a comprehensive center for mission in the Midwest, alongside secondary schools, a college, and a cathedral. Western Seminary had chosen its name as an effort to be a regional, "general" seminary for the Midwest. The creation of Seabury-Western in 1933 was seen as bringing together high church and low church parties to provide for a single, unified, regional midwestern seminary to serve the church. Bexley Hall was founded as an outgrowth of Philander Chase's conviction that there needed to be a seminary on the frontier to serve the needs of the church on the frontier. Its relocation to Rochester in 1968 was an effort to respond to changing needs in the church, and becoming part of an urban, ecumenical consortium was an effort to adapt to these changes. Certainly, both seminaries were facing financial and enrollment challenges. But those were not the only motivating factors; those involved also understood that The Episcopal Church was changing, theological education was changing, and the seminaries were being called to adapt again to these changes as they had previously. Discussions around a deeper, federated partnership were seen as another step in living out these founding visions. In February of 2011, a joint operating agreement was signed, the first formal step in a developing partnership. There was a single interim president for both institutions, along with combined efforts in fundraising and development, while all courses were open to students from both seminaries. These were steps toward a closer partnership, collaborating in some areas while still retaining separate accreditation, faculties, degree offerings, and boards of trustees.

The first major commitments toward federation came in the spring 2012 board of trustees meeting, when two steps were taken. First, the two boards of trustees voted to create a single, federated entity, Bexley Seabury Seminary Federation. As with most seminary partnerships, the name was chosen carefully.[2] The legal name chosen was Bexley Hall Seabury-Western Theological Seminary Federation (with the hyphen included) so that the full names of both schools—Bexley Hall and Seabury-Western Theological Seminary—were included in order to be sure that the new entity would be the legal continuation of the predecessor bodies. "Federation" was also specifically chosen to indicate a collaborative partnership and was a deliberate avoidance of an indication of merger or of one school subsuming the other. Going forward, while the legal name was Bexley Hall Seabury-Western Theological Seminary Federation, the seminary would generally use Bexley Seabury or Bexley Seabury Seminary Federation in day-to-day communications. Next, at the same meeting where both boards voted to enter into the federation, Roger Ferlo, at the time associate dean and director of the Institute of Christian Formation and Leadership at Virginia Theological Seminary, was called as president. Notably, Ferlo was clear that he would only accept the call as president if the two seminaries had already voted to federate. As with the formation of Seabury-Western in 1933, following the vote to create the federation, there came the more detailed processes of bringing together different faculties, programs, boards of trustees, and institutional histories and cultures.

To provide for this, Bexley Seabury created a flexible and innovative model. A new not-for-profit educational corporation was created, the aforementioned Bexley Hall Seabury-Western Theological Seminary Federation, with a board of directors.[3]

2. For instance, minutes from the 1933 discussions specifically state that there should be a hyphen between Seabury and Western in the name of the new institution to denote equality, thus giving us Seabury-Western.

3. The term "board of trustees" has been used in this history to refer to the governing bodies of Bexley Hall and Seabury-Western prior to 2012. Given changes in not-for-profit law in various states, when Bexley Seabury Seminary Federation was created in 2012, the language used in the state of Illinois had

Seabury-Western Theological Seminary and Bexley Hall Seminary continued legally to exist, but as wholly owned subsidiaries of Bexley Hall Seabury-Western Seminary Federation. The individuals comprising the board of directors of BSSF also served as the board of directors for the subsidiaries Bexley Hall and Seabury-Western. BSSF, in effect, functioned as a kind of educational holding company. This was done for several reasons. For one, there was a real concern over the perception that one seminary was acquiring another. There is a long history in theological education in North America of one seminary "winning" a merger, with one school being absorbed into another. There is a history of this in The Episcopal Church, for instance, with concerns raised with the 1974 merger of Philadelphia Divinity School and Episcopal Theological School that the history and legacy of PDS was largely forgotten.

This structure was also chosen for practical reasons: Seabury-Western and Bexley Hall were legally incorporated not-for-profit educational institutions and also were accredited by the Association of Theological Schools and licensed to function and to grant degrees by, respectively, the Illinois Board of Higher Education and the Ohio Board of Regents, and recognized by the US Department of Education for participation in federal student loan programs and for being able to issue visas for international students. Keeping the legally incorporated structures in place ensured there would be no disruptions or issues with accessing endowment or restricted funds held in the names of Seabury-Western and Bexley Hall or participation in any federal programs, since the predecessor bodies continued to exist.

Prior changes in location or status for both institutions had raised these concerns. For instance, in 1933, several Bishop Seabury Divinity School trustees wondered if the restricted funds held for that school could be put in use by a new, merged entity. In 1968, there had been some tension determining which restricted funds would become the property of Bexley Hall and which would

---

changed to board of directors. Accordingly, when Bexley Seabury was formed, the new governing body was called the board of directors, which will be the nomenclature used after 2012.

remain with Kenyon College, which at times came down to parsing the terms used in restricted bequests.[4] In the newly created BSSF, the subsidiaries Seabury-Western Theological Seminary and Bexley Hall Seminary were declared to be the legal successors of all prior incorporated entities, which allowed not only for continued access to prior restricted funds, but for any potential pending bequests. As late as 2014, when I was academic dean, an estate attorney contacted me, stating that he was the estate attorney for a bequest designated for Bexley Hall Seminary. The will had been drafted in the 1960s, so Gambier, Ohio, was given as the address and Kenyon had been initially contacted. Kenyon College responded by stating that Bexley Hall no longer existed, and it was only through a Google search the attorney was able to contact me as academic dean. Since BSSF had retained Bexley Hall's legal incorporation, and declared it to be the successor of prior entities, the bequest was able to be smoothly transferred to BSSF. Further, by keeping these entities legally incorporated, this allowed for maintaining existing authority to operate and grant degrees in Illinois and Ohio until BSSF could receive accreditation by the Association of Theological Schools and then seek licensure in Illinois and Ohio for the new entity. As a result of the formation of BSSF, the Association of Theological Schools scheduled a special, focused visit in May of 2013, resulting in the approval by ATS to combine the two separate accreditations into a single accreditation for BSSF, with a more detailed, comprehensive visit scheduled for 2015.

From 2012 to 2016, Bexley Seabury Seminary Federation offered two degrees—the doctor of ministry[5] and the master of di-

---

4. For the issues concerning the Bishop Seabury restricted funds, see discussion in chapter 2. This issue was resolved by keeping the restricted funds held by Bishop Seabury Divinity School under the control of the Diocese of Minnesota, but by stipulating those funds would be used in support of Seabury-Western Theological Seminary. With regard to the restricted funds designated for Bexley Hall, see discussion in chapter 3.

5. In congregational development through BSSF and in preaching through the Association of Chicago Theological Schools. The DMin in congregational development was also, for a number of years in the late 2000s and

vinity—along with a Diploma in Anglican Studies at two different campus locations in Chicago and in Columbus, Ohio. While there were two locations, there was a single board of directors, a single faculty, a single student body, and a single curriculum. The DMin was offered primarily, but not exclusively, at the Chicago campus; similarly, the master of divinity was offered primarily, but not entirely, at the Columbus campus. There were DMin courses offered in Columbus, and MDiv courses offered in Chicago. Courses in the Diploma in Anglican Studies, primarily intended for persons enrolled in another seminary or who already had an MDiv, were offered across both sites and online. During this 2012–2016 period, the MDiv program was primarily a residential program, while the Diploma in Anglican Studies and DMin were low-residency programs, with courses primarily online or offered through short-term intensives in January or June, or during the semester over three weekends.

A significant challenge facing BSSF was communicating these changes and the vision for the Federation to the church as a whole and with its alumni. A significant cohort of Seabury-Western alumni were shocked if not angered by the decision to declare exigency, suspend the MDiv program, and sell the Sheridan Road campus to Northwestern University. The impact of this can be seen with the steep decline in giving by alumni after the declaration of exigency. There was a commonly held perception in The Episcopal Church at that time that Seabury-Western had closed. Bexley Hall had a similar, though not entirely parallel, challenge with its alumni and with its perception in The Episcopal Church. Bexley's relocations from 1968 to 1999 had left it with different cohorts of alumni: those who were primarily affiliated with Gambier and Kenyon; those from the Rochester years and affiliated with CRCDS; and a growing group of alumni whose primary experience of Bexley was as part of the Columbus-based, Trinity Lutheran ecumenical partnership. It was a challenge holding together and finding common ground among disparate groups of alumni who, in some

---

early 2010s, offered jointly with the Church Divinity School of the Pacific before CDSP eventually declined to renew the partnership.

ways, had very different experiences of Bexley. Equally challenging was addressing concerns that alumni not be left behind or marginalized with the formation of the new Federation. As President Ferlo commented, "A challenge was convincing the church and alumni Seabury-Western was still alive, and that Bexley had finally found some stability."[6]

As the Federation came into being, ongoing conversations concerned long-term sustainability, specifically whether it would or even could continue to operate on two locations. There were several factors that went into those conversations. One was financial: while the seminary owned no property, and thus had no maintenance issues, it did rent space, and two campus locations meant paying rent to two different partners. Another factor involved institutional capacity: two locations meant maintaining two state licensing authorizations and all of the institutional efforts and bandwidth involved in that maintenance. In a report to the board of directors, the academic dean provided important perspective by noting, "There are no two-degree, two-location, ATS-accredited seminaries that are BSSF's size, because of the institutional capacity required to do so."[7] Throughout the 2012–2016 period, there were ongoing discussions about whether it would be best to consolidate operations in a single location, and, if so, where and how.

These conversations were wide ranging and explored a number of options. The board and leadership considered consolidation in Columbus through the existing partnership with Trinity Lutheran, or perhaps with the other member of the Theological Consortium of Greater Columbus, the Methodist Theological School in Ohio, located just outside the city of Columbus. There were preliminary conversations held with other member schools of the Association of Chicago Theological Schools and other Episcopal seminaries. The decision to leave Columbus and the partnership with Trinity Lutheran Seminary was a difficult one. The Trinity-Bexley Seabury partnership had been the most collaborative and

---

6. Interview with Roger Ferlo, February 25, 2024.

7. Academic Dean's Report to Board of Directors, October 2016. Personal papers of Academic Dean Thomas Ferguson.

integrated venture in theological education between the ELCA and The Episcopal Church. An additional factor in this decision had to do with Trinity Lutheran's own internal developments. Trinity had been struggling with its own financial and enrollment challenges and was looking at different options and possibilities for its own future. As noted in chapter 3, a number of seminaries in the ELCA were examining different forms of affiliation and partnership. In the decade from 2010 to 2019, some seminaries merged with another seminary, while others merged with ELCA-affiliated universities. Trinity would eventually make the decision to merge back with Capital University, from which it had become independent in the early 1960s. While BSSF was included in Trinity's initial conversations with Capital, there was still concern about what it would mean to be in a partnership not with an independent, freestanding ELCA seminary but with a university. Having an educational partner was essential for BSSF: the Federation did not have the resources necessary to achieve ATS accreditation on its own—BSSF had no Scripture courses, for instance—and was able to offer the MDiv through affiliation with another ATS accredited school who were able to provide the resources BSSF could not.

The proposal presented to the board of directors in the spring of 2016 was to cease instruction at the Columbus site and relocate operations to the campus of Chicago Theological Seminary (CTS), affiliated with the United Church of Christ and located in the Hyde Park neighborhood of Chicago. There were several reasons for this choice. CTS had moved into a new, fully accessible, LEED Gold Certified environmentally sustainable building. The location in Hyde Park allowed for closer cooperation and collaboration with a plurality of the ACTS members (McCormick Theological Seminary, Lutheran School of Theology in Chicago, Catholic Theological Union, CTS) and the University of Chicago Divinity School, all nearby in the Hyde Park neighborhood. CTS had already transitioned to a low-residency program of study for its master of divinity and had the infrastructure in place for delivery of content through online and short-term, intensive residential courses. Since BSSF was transitioning to a low-residency model, and since MDiv students would need to take courses through any potential partner, it was important to have a partner with a similar low-residency program. In addition, CTS had an intentional commitment to diversity as well as to forming ecumenical and interreligious partnerships, which aligned with BSSF's sustained commitment to ecumenical collaboration.[8]

Beginning in the fall of 2016, BSSF engaged in another relocation—since 2007, this would be the fifth campus location[9]—and transitioned from a mostly residential MDiv to an entirely low-residency program to complement its existing low-residency and online DMin and Diploma in Anglican Studies courses. This consolidation allowed BSSF to commit itself to its core values and commitments in theological education: to be a center for theological education that was diverse, accessible, collaborative, and mission oriented.

The transition to a low-residential and online curriculum allowed for increased accessibility to theological education. While a residential model has its advantages, it also has its own set of barriers: people have family and work commitments, and a residential model in essence necessitates several moves over a three-year period. This transition saw increases in student enrollment, especially in the MDiv program. In the 2010–2015 period, there were an average of thirteen to fifteen full-time students enrolled in total in the residential MDiv. In the 2020s, that number had doubled, with an average of over thirty students enrolled in the program. Theological education had changed significantly over the years, and both seminaries had done so as well: from the initial tutorial model to accommodating married students to making changes to incorporate commuter students, to developing short-term intensive courses for partner dioceses. The shift to low residency was another incarnation of Bexley Hall and Seabury-Western's

---

8. For example, at the time, CTS was one of the few ATS accredited seminaries that had a tenure-track professor of Islamic studies.

9. Evanston (relocated to ELCA Church Center in 2012), Rochester (campus closed in 2008), Columbus (campus closed 2016), ELCA Churchwide Center (2012–2016).

adaptation to changes in both theological education and in The Episcopal Church.

BSSF also has engaged in a sustained process of commitment to diversity. As this history has shown, Bexley Hall and Seabury-Western have been historically rooted in whiteness and have at times reflected and replicated the marginalization of non-white, male, straight communities and constituencies. With the formation of BSSF came a commitment to living into diversity. Prior to 2016, the community was overwhelmingly white in terms of faculty, staff, and students. By 2022, this commitment to diversity was showing its fruits: nearly 21 percent of the student body consisted of students of color and 50 percent consisted of women students.[10] A dedicated scholarship for LGBTQ persons, the St. Marina Scholarship, was established through the support of anonymous donors to provide a full scholarship for "an entering first-year Master of Divinity student who identifies as LGBTQ and who demonstrates a strong commitment to pursuing justice ministry as an ordained person in The Episcopal Church."[11] This commitment to diversity is reflected as well in curriculum redesign and development. Each course in the redeveloped curriculum is required to address "racism, white supremacy/privilege/normativity, as well violence against BIPOC bodies in a way that broadens students' encounter with the discipline of the course" and to incorporate "how the course will attend to issues of difference and diversity" in its learning methodology.[12]

BSSF has also taken steps to begin to address some of the issues concerning complicity with marginalization of Native peoples, which, as we have seen in this history, is woven throughout the history particularly of the Seabury-Western legacy of the Federation. BSSF has created a competency-based master of

---

10. Association of Theological Schools, "Evaluation Committee Report for Comprehensive Evaluation Visit for Reaffirmation of Accreditation," 7; Bexley Seabury Seminary Federation Archives.

11. Bexley Seabury, "St. Marina Scholarship."

12. Bexley Seabury Seminary Federation required syllabus template for all courses.

divinity program, an additional pathway alongside the more traditional course-based MDiv degree. A competency-based program is not necessarily based on taking coursework: rather, objectives and goals are set for all of the components of the master of divinity, and students work with mentors to devise ways to fulfill and demonstrate competency in those objectives. This could be done in a variety of ways, including taking some courses, or by directed study, or by project-based learning, or by recognizing competencies the student might already have coming into the program. The competency-based MDiv is part of the continued efforts by BSSF to increase accessibility for theological education and formation. Yet by also incorporating and acknowledging different students' experiences and competencies, this is also an effort to provide theological education and formation for historically marginalized communities. In the initial pilot program, nearly half of the students enrolled are from Native American communities, and the seminary has engaged a professor of Indigenous studies who is an enrolled Blackfeet tribal member to assist in developing the program. The development of the competency-based MDiv program is an intentional effort to live into Bexley Seabury's historic commitment to provide theological education for Native American and Indigenous communities, and to do so by learning from past complicity with white supremacy and cultural genocide by doing so in cooperation and collaboration with Native peoples and communities.

A distinctive aspect of BSSF's commitment to being mission based is represented by the innovative redevelopment of the field education component of the MDiv degree. Previously, the field education component of Bexley Seabury's MDiv was based—like a good number of MDiv programs, both at Episcopal seminaries and non-Episcopal seminaries—on a one- or two-semester internship in a local ministry setting, overseen by an onsite mentor, and combined with a didactic component (usually a field education seminar or equivalent). As the seminary transitioned to a low-residency program, with an emphasis on being mission oriented, the field education program was redeveloped as Communities of Learning and Formation. Rather than being a one- or two-course sequence, integration of learning and practicum takes place throughout the length of the seminary program as students take five courses over two and a half years of the MDiv program. Learning, integration, and reflection take place in a student's sponsoring congregation or other local setting, combined with coursework through the seminary. The Communities of Learning and Formation program also helps BSSF live into its commitment to collaboration, by forming partnerships with local congregations, dioceses, and mentors. This has been essential to this transition to a low-residency model, and the Communities of Learning and Formation program was noted by the Association of Theological Schools as "in many ways the heart of the MDiv program."[13]

As part of being a "Seminary Beyond Walls," BSSF also intentionally is committed to collaboration. All too often a seminary has been where someone is sent to, becomes part of for a number of years, and, upon completion of a program, is sent to a third place to begin ministry. Transitioning to a low-residency program for the master of divinity necessitated developing more collaborative partnerships with constituencies throughout the church, since students would be engaging in so much of their program while remaining in their local dioceses and local congregations. By 2024, Bexley Seabury's student body included students from twenty-two different dioceses, harkening back to the 1960s and 1970s when both Seabury-Western's and Bexley Hall's student bodies were at their most broadly representative of the church as a whole. This emphasis on collaboration is also seen through intentional efforts to collaborate in theological education and formation. The Pathways for Baptismal Living program was established to continue to live into the call to provide theological education and formation for all the baptized that had been integral in the creation of SeaburyNext. In addition to providing opportunities for learning and enrichment, the Pathways program also has developed training programs for licensed lay ministries (such as Licensed Preacher)

---

13. Association of Theological Schools, "Evaluation Committee Report," 11; Bexley Seabury Seminary Federation Archives.

and a course of study for persons preparing for the vocational diaconate. The Diploma in Anglican Studies program, which is primarily intended for students enrolled at other seminaries or enrolled in diocesan training programs, has involved building partnerships with diocesan training programs and non-Episcopal seminaries.

In 2017, President Roger Ferlo retired after leading the Federation through a transformative five years. An innovative structure led to the blending and creation of a single board of directors, consolidated on a single site, with a single curriculum, faculty, and staff. An important milestone in 2015 came when the Association of Theological Schools granted accreditation to Bexley Seabury Seminary Federation, by virtue of its collaborative arrangement with Chicago Theological Seminary. In 2018, the Rev. Dr. Micah Jackson was called as president. The Federation continued to grow its programs and student body as it lived into being a fully low-residency seminary. As the Federation moved toward its reaccreditation in 2022, an important missional and strategic decision was made: to pursue accreditation without the necessity of needing to be affiliated with another educational institution. This had been part of Bexley Hall since 1968, when it moved to Rochester, and had been part of the Federation since its formation in 2012. Sole accreditation meant the investment in resources to be able to provide the entire breadth of offerings needed to offer the master of divinity degree. There were several reasons for pursuing sole accreditation. The primary reason was missional and pedagogical. Accreditation through partnership with another institution meant that students took up to half their courses somewhere else, while sole accreditation allowed for the student experience better to reflect the seminary's commitments by taking the majority of their program through BSSF. There were also financial reasons: the funds paid to another institution as part of an affiliated relationship were instead invested in adding faculty resources in Scripture, liturgy, church history, and preaching.

As Bexley Seabury Seminary Federation entered its bicentennial year in 2024, it stood in its strongest position in years. It had a settled location and sole accreditation, was increasingly more diverse, and had its largest student body, faculty, and staff in over twenty years. BSSF had weathered its challenges and chosen to adapt to significant changes that were sweeping over both higher education in North America and The Episcopal Church. Having survived, adapted, and even begun flourishing, Bexley Seabury has the opportunity to decide how to live into this new incarnation.

The various founders of Bexley Seabury's predecessor schools often spoke of the need for institutions on the "frontier." This language was used by Philander Chase, James Lloyd Breck, Benjamin Whipple, and by the founders of Western Seminary in Chicago. Yet this language is problematic: notions of "frontier" were essential to cultural and literal genocide of Native and indigenous peoples and reflect a colonial, exploitative, settler perspective. While this language is used at times in this history, it is predominantly within the historical context used by the various founders. Bexley Seabury now speaks of its calling to be a seminary "beyond walls." Originally this phrase was meant to capture the ways in which Bexley Seabury was moving into a low-residency model and the ways that learning and formation no longer took place predominantly within a classroom located on a campus. Yet throughout this history, we have seen how those walls of the classroom were not only physical walls. Bexley Seabury's walls historically excluded women, Native peoples, African Americans, openly LGBTQIA+ persons, and others. Only in recent years has Bexley Seabury begun any kind of process for naming and addressing these actions of historic exclusion and marginalization. Acknowledgment of past injustice is an important first step, and this bicentennial history is intended to be part of that acknowledgment. But any process toward justice requires actionable, tangible steps.

As Bexley Seabury stands on the threshold of its third century, there is the opportunity truly to live into this vision. By not only moving "beyond walls" but to continue to remove the walls that reinforce systemic injustice and division. To look to the vision of Jesus as described by the author of the Letter to the Ephesians, who not only moves beyond walls, but is a redeemer who "is our peace . . . and who has broken down the dividing wall, that is, the hostility between us."[14]

---

14. Ephesians 2:14.

Afterword

By The Rev. Canon C. K. Robertson, PhD
Canon and Senior Advisor to the Presiding Bishop
of The Episcopal Church

As Dr. Yamada rightly pointed out in the book's foreword, in these early decades of the twenty-first century we are witnessing profound changes in theological education—in terms of financial models, delivery systems, and student demographics—all in the context of shifts in both higher education and religious practice in North America. In light of these changing realities, this new and updated history of Bexley Seabury has proven to be not only timely but, as Dr. Ferguson notes in his introduction, long overdue. The resulting exploration of the various twists and turns in the journey of the institutions that would eventually become today's Federation provides both inspiration and challenge to us today.

It is no exaggeration to say that robust theological education, and its role in the formation of ordained and lay leaders, is critical to the long-term health and vitality of The Episcopal Church. Of course, there is nothing new about this, nor is this somehow unique to our Church. A century ago, following the devastation of the so-called War to End All Wars, bishops from throughout the worldwide Anglican Communion gathered together for the sixth Lambeth Conference. Amid their urgent appeal for building relationships with other Christians, seeking not uniformity but rather affirming diversity of thought and practice, they highlighted the importance of theological education as a foundational piece in "making room for the Spirit to work."

In more recent years, during my own travels throughout the various national or regional provinces that comprise the Communion, I have asked Church leaders what they see as some of the greatest needs or challenges they face. In each and every instance, one of the first things they mention is theological education and formation! In our own Church, both the presiding bishop and members of the House of Bishops have acknowledged the changes already discussed and voiced their commitment to collaborate with seminary deans and presidents, and other providers of theological training, reexamining what is needed to move forward in today's work of mission and ministry. As it has in the past, Bexley Seabury is again part of that forward-facing work.

In a letter written in 1675 to his colleague Richard Hooke, Sir Isaac Newton famously said, "If I have seen further, it is by standing on the shoulders of giants."[1] As this book has reminded us, an honest appraisal of the past reveals more complex realities than we often have wanted to admit, and even giants can be all too human. But by tapping into our collective history, we can dare to take the baton that has been handed to us from all those faithful and fallible souls who came before us, and now, in the words of the Letter to the Hebrews (12:1), "run with perseverance the race set before us." There are chapters yet to be written in the story of this Seminary Beyond Walls, and indeed in the larger Church and Communion, the body of Christ in the world. The mission continues, and future histories will take into account the decisions we make and the things we do now.

---

1. Newton, "Letter from Sir Isaac Newton to Robert Hooke."

Bibliography

Anderson, David Wallace. *Education for Extinction: Native Americans and the Boarding School Experience*. Lawrence: University of Kansas Press, 1995.

Anderson, Owanah. *Four Hundred Years: Anglican/Episcopal Mission Among American Indians*. Cincinnati: Forward Movement, 1997.

———. "Native American Seminary Enrollment Increasing." *Episcopal News Service*, Apr. 13, 1989. Episcopal Church Digital Archives. https://digitalarchives.episcopalarchives.org/cgi-bin/ENS/ENSpress_release.pl?pr_number=89073.

Bass, Diana Butler. *Standing Against the Whirlwind: Evangelical Episcopalians in 19th Century America*. New York: Oxford University Press, 1995.

Bexley Seabury Seminary. "St. Marina Scholarship: Honoring Diversity in Ministry." https://www.bexleyseabury.edu/bexley-seabury-st-marina-scholarship/.

Bexley Seabury Seminary Federation Archives. Bexley Hall Seabury-Western Seminary Federation, Chicago, Illinois.

Bragg, George Freeman. *History of the Afro-American Group in The Episcopal Church*. Baltimore: Church Advocate, 1922.

Breck, Charles. *The Life of the Reverend James Lloyd Breck*. New York: E. & J. B. Young, 1886.

Chase, Philander. *Bishop Chase's Reminiscences*. Vol. 1. Boston: James Dow, 1848.

Cochran, Mary E. *Dakota Cross Bearer: The Life and World of a Native American Bishop*. Lincoln: University of Nebraska Press, 2000.

General Convention. *Journal of the General Convention of The Episcopal Church*. The Episcopal Church, 1970.

———. *Journal of the General Convention of...The Episcopal Church, Philadelphia, 1997*. New York: General Convention, 1998. Episcopal Archives. https://digitalarchives.episcopalarchives.org/cgi-bin/acts/acts_resolution.pl?resolution=1997-A053.

Episcopal Church Indigenous Ministries. "Doctrine of Discovery Resources." https://www.episcopalchurch.org/category/doctrine-of-discovery/.

BIBLIOGRAPHY

An Episcopal Glossary of the Church, "Conscience Clause." https://www.episcopalchurch.org/glossary/conscience-clause/.

Gundersen, Joan. "An Experiment in 'Christian Co-operation': Seabury Divinity School and Carleton College." *Anglican and Episcopal History* 56:4 (Dec. 1987) 444–54.

Haugaard, William. "The Missionary Vision of James Lloyd Breck in Minnesota." *Historical Magazine of the Protestant Episcopal Church* 54:3 (Sept. 1985) 241–51.

An Illustrated Historical Sketch of the Western Theological Seminary. Chicago: N.P., ca. 1915.

Jay, William. "Letter to C.P. McIlvaine." Kenyon College Archives, November 17, 1855. https://digital.kenyon.edu/mcilvaine_letters/5/.

Johnson, Russell. "A History of Seabury-Western Seminary." Unpublished manuscript, Bexley Seabury Seminary Archives.

Kenyon College. "Catalogue of Kenyon College, Gambier, Ohio. 1892-1893." *Kenyon College Course Catalogs* 57. https://digital.kenyon.edu/cgi/viewcontent.cgi?article=1055&context=coursecatalogs.

Lutheran-Episcopal Dialogue. "An Agreement of Full Communion: Called to Common Mission." The Episcopal Church, Aug. 19, 1999. https://www.episcopalchurch.org/ministries/ecumenical-interreligious/agreement-of-full-communion-called-to-common-mission/.

McElwain, Frank, Percy Norwood, and Frederick Grant. "Seabury Western Theological Seminary: A History." *Historical Magazine of the Protestant Episcopal Church* 5:4 (Dec. 1936) 286–311.

Miller, Glenn. *Piety and Intellect: The Aims and Purposes of Antebellum Theological Education.* Atlanta: Scholars, 1990.

———. *Piety and Profession: American Protestant Theological Education, 1870–1970.* Grand Rapids: Eerdmans, 2007.

Newton, Isaac. "Letter from Sir Isaac Newton to Robert Hooke." Pennsylvania Historical Society.

Niebuhr, H. Richard. *The Purpose of the Church in Its Ministry: Reflections on the Aims of Theological Education.* New York: Harper & Row, 1956.

Noble, John. "A Portrait of Bishop Keeler." *The Living Church* 129:7 (Aug. 15, 1954) 13–14. https://www.google.com/books/edition/The_Living_Church/m2XkAAAAMAAJ?hl=en&gbpv=1&bsq=Portrait.

"Seventy Years of Seabury Divinity School." *Seabury Divinity School Bulletin* 10:4 (Dec. 1927).

Smith, Newland. "Doctrine of Discovery Lament Offering 2: Recognition of 'Our' Places in the Story." Episcopal Church Indigenous Ministries, Nov. 27, 2012. https://www.episcopalchurch.org/indigenousministries/doctrine-of-discovery-lament-offering-2-recognition-of-our-places-in-the-story/.

Smith, Richard. *Bishop McIlvaine, Slavery, Britain, and the Civil War.* Bloomington, IN: Xlibris, 2014.

Bibliography

Spielmann, Richard. *Bexley Hall, 150 Years: A Brief History.* Rochester, NY: Colgate Rochester Divinity School, 1974.

Whipple, Henry. *Light and Shadows of a Long Episcopate.* New York: Macmillan, 1902.

Wikipedia. "Demographics of Chicago." https://en.wikipedia.org/wiki/Demographics_of_Chicago.

———. "Faribault, Minnesota." https://en.wikipedia.org/wiki/Faribault,_Minnesota.

———. "Saint Paul, Minnesota." https://en.wikipedia.org/wiki/Saint_Paul,_Minnesota.

Wisconsin Department of Public Instruction. "Oneida Nation." https://dpi.wi.gov/amind/tribalnationswi/oneida.

www.ingramcontent.com/pod-product-compliance
Lightning Source LLC
Chambersburg PA
CBHW050838160426
43192CB00011B/2068